SHOP FRONTS

# SHOP FRONTS

Jacques Debaigts

Photos by Michel Nahmias

Architectural Book Publishing Co., New York

729.1
D286

Published by Architectural Book Publishing Co., Inc., New York
Library of Congress Catalog Card Number: 74 – 18270
International Standard Book No. 0 – 8038 – 0236 – 6

English translation: J. A. Underwood
Layout: Studio S + T, Lausanne
Plans: Bruno Huber
© Copyright 1974 by the Office du Livre S.A., Fribourg, Switzerland

Printed in Switzerland

Sommaire            Inhalt            Contents

DEVANTURES     SCHAUFENSTER     SHOP FRONTS

# Devantures

« C'était, dans sa fraîcheur gaie, un vaste développement d'architecture polychrome, rehaussée d'or, annonçant le vacarme et l'éclat du commerce intérieur, accrochant les yeux comme un gigantesque étalage qui aurait flambé des couleurs les plus vives. Au rez-de-chaussée, pour ne pas tuer les étoffes des vitrines, la décoration restait sobre: un soubassement en marbre vert de mer; les piles d'angles et les piliers d'appui recouverts de marbre noir, dont la sévérité s'éclairait de cartouches dorés; et le reste en glace sans tain, dans les châssis de fer, rien que des glaces qui semblaient ouvrir les profondeurs des galeries et des halls au plein jour de la rue. Mais, à mesure que les étalages montaient, s'allumaient les tons éclatants. La frise du rez-de-chaussée déroulait des mosaïques, une guirlande de fleurs rouges et bleues, alternées avec des plaques de marbre, où étaient gravés des noms de marchandises, à l'infini, ceignant le colosse. »

Emile Zola
*Au Bonheur des Dames* (1883)

C'est l'aube de l'ère industrielle qui marque le grand tournant fonctionnel, esthétique et sociologique du commerce. En cela, le texte d'Emile Zola qui ouvre cet exposé est assez significatif. En effet, les lieux de vente construits auparavant n'ont évolué que très lentement dans leur structure architecturale. Intégrés le plus souvent à l'habitation, il ne pouvait en être autrement.
Au XIXe siècle — tout au moins en Europe —, le lieu commercial, le magasin — à commencer par sa façade — devient un théâtre où, à l'action vitale d'acheter, s'ajoute celle plus prosaïque de se distraire, s'inspirant en cela de certaines époques où commerce et fête étaient étroitement mêlés.

## LES BUTS, LES PROBLÈMES

Un magasin contemporain doit, par conséquent, offrir au client une atmosphère gaie, détendue, sinon euphorisante, où le commerçant s'efforcera de présenter sa marchandise dans des conditions optimales de mise en valeur. Le décor, les matériaux, la lumière ont une importance prépondérante en affirmant une distribution du mobilier spécifique au commerce concerné et une circulation logique des visiteurs et du personnel.
L'aménagement d'un magasin, petit ou grand, est une affaire de spécialiste. Avant d'être charmé par

# Schaufenster

« In ihrer strahlenden Frische bot die Fassade eine breite Entfaltung polychromer, durch Gold betonter Architektur, die den Lärm und den Glanz des Handels im Inneren ankündigte und wie eine riesige, in den lebhaftesten Farben flammende Auslage die Blicke fesselte. Im Erdgeschoß war, um nicht die Stoffe in den Schaufenstern um ihre Wirkung zu bringen, die Dekoration nüchtern gehalten: ein Sockel aus meergrünem Marmor; die Pilaster und die Stützpfeiler mit schwarzem Marmor verkleidet, dessen Ernst vergoldete Zierleisten aufhellten; und alles übrige bestand aus Spiegelglas in eisernen Fassungen, nichts als Glasscheiben, die die Tiefen der Galerien und Hallen dem vollen, von der Straße hereindringenden Tageslicht aufzutun schienen. Doch je höher die Stockwerke emporstiegen, um so leuchtendere Farben glühten auf. Der Fries des Erdgeschosses, der sich endlos, rings um den ganzen Koloß, hinzog, zeigte Mosaiken, ein Gewinde roter und blauer Blumen, in regelmäßigen Abständen von Marmorplatten unterbrochen, auf denen Warenbezeichungen eingeschnitten waren. »

Emile Zola
*Paradies der Damen* (1883)

Der Beginn des Industriezeitalters ist in funktioneller, ästhetischer und soziologischer Hinsicht der große Wendepunkt im Bereich des Handels. Der diesen Ausführungen vorangestellte Text von Emile Zola ist dafür recht bezeichnend. Die Verkaufsräume von früher haben sich in ihrer architektonischen Struktur nur sehr langsam entwickelt, da sie fast immer in den Wohnbereich miteinbezogen waren.
Im 19. Jahrhundert wird der Umschlagplatz des Handels, das Geschäft — zumindest in Europa — von außen gesehen zu einem öffentlichen Schauplatz, an dem neben der lebenswichtigen Tätigkeit des Kaufens zugleich das Vergnügen seinen Platz fand, in Anlehnung an bestimmte Epochen, da Handel und Volksfest eng miteinander verbunden waren.

## ZIELE UND PROBLEME

Infolgedessen muß ein Geschäft dem Kunden heute eine heitere, entspannte und anregende Atmosphäre bieten, wobei sich der Geschäftsinhaber darum bemüht, seine Ware unter optimalen Bedingungen zur Geltung zu bringen. Dekoration, Ma-

# Shop Fronts

' It was a vast, variegated architectural panorama, all gaiety and freshness, set off with touches of gold, heralding the din and brilliance of the commerce conducted within, drawing the eye like some gigantic display ablaze with all the most dazzling colours of the spectrum. The ground-floor façade, lest it detract from the materials on show in the windows, was restrained: the base of sea-green marble; the corner piers and supporting members clad in stately black marble relieved by gilt cartouches; the rest plate glass, nothing but sheets of plate glass mounted in iron frames, seeming to bathe the farthest depths of gallery and hall in the bright daylight of the street. As the eye travelled upward, however, it encountered ever more luminous hues. The ground-floor frieze showed a mosaic of garlands of red and blue flowers alternating with slabs of marble engraved with the names of the different wares, forming a continuous belt that girded the whole colossus. '

Emile Zola
*Au Bonheur des Dames* (1883)

It was the dawn of the industrial age that marked the great functional, aesthetic, and sociological turning-point in the development of commerce. This is the significance of Zola's description of Octave Mouret's vast and splendid Paris department store. Prior to that period the architecture of commercial premises evolved very slowly. Trade being generally conducted in the home, things could hardly have been otherwise.
In the course of the nineteenth century—at least in Europe—the shop, and particularly the shop front, became a theatre in which to the essential activity of making purchases was added the secondary activity of finding entertainment—an association that had its roots in periods when trade had been closely bound up with popular festivals.

## OBJECTIVES AND PROBLEMS

The modern shop must consequently offer the customer a cheerful atmosphere that will induce relaxation and even a positive feeling of well-being and in which the shopkeeper will do all in his power to present his merchandise in the most favourable conditions possible. Decor, materials, and lighting are of capital importance in deciding on a furnishing layout appropriate to the particular

le décor intérieur, il est logique, sinon indispensable, que l'acheteur potentiel, le passant, soient sollicités afin d'en franchir le seuil. La présentation des produits en vitrine reste la plus évidente des sollicitations, bien que ce ne soit pas toujours le cas, ni le besoin.

Ainsi, l'architecture de la façade peut devenir signal, affiche, synthèse du produit ou de l'activité commerciale sans pour autant les mettre en lumière.

De l'immense glace claire, mettant le magasin en contact direct avec la rue, à la façade aveugle, percée d'accès discrets, la gamme des solutions architecturales est vaste. De toute façon, le choix d'un type de façade dépend, avec plus ou moins d'acuité, de la confrontation des contingences suivantes:

— le type de commerce et de produit vendu;
— la politique commerciale: clientèle populaire, de luxe, snob, etc.;
— la nature du produit vendu, son aspect, sa qualité;
— la concurrence;
— les obligations architecturales: intégration à l'immeuble dans lequel s'inscrit le magasin (édifices classés ou très caractéristiques), et au site construit.

Bien que ces contingences forment un tout, nous allons analyser chacune d'elles séparément pour en tirer un profit.

*Le type de commerce et de produit vendu*
Un bijou ne se présente pas de la même façon qu'un bagage ou qu'une motocyclette. Si le genre de la clientèle est différent pour chaque produit, ce dernier possède en outre des dimensions qui lui sont propres, déterminant d'une façon plus ou moins impérative le caractère de la façade et la particularité des vitrines. Deux solutions se présentent:
— Le vitrage total:
Il offre une surface d'exposition importante, mais nécessite, selon le volume des objets proposés, une subdivision au niveau des modules de présentation qui se trouvent à l'intérieur et qui peuvent être réalisés lors de l'équipement et de la décoration du magasin.
— La subdivision dans la conception architecturale de la façade:
Cette solution, la plus audacieuse, affirme indéniablement le ton et le caractère du commerce. Elle stimule et intrigue le passant comme le ferait une sculpture, un bas-relief contemporain, puis l'attire vers une présentation parfaitement adaptée au produit.

terial, Beleuchtung sind von entscheidender Bedeutung; die Einrichtung muß für den betreffenden Geschäftstyp charakteristisch sein und zu einem logisch ablaufenden Verkehrsfluß von Kundschaft und Personal beitragen.

Die innere und äußere Gestaltung eines Geschäfts, ob groß oder klein, ist Sache des Spezialisten, denn der potentielle Käufer, der Passant muß erst einmal dazu gebracht werden, die Schwelle zu überschreiten. Die Schaufensterauslage ist der offensichtlichste Anreiz dazu, obwohl dieses Mittel auch entbehrlich sein kann. Die Architektur der Geschäftsfassade kann daher zum Signal, Plakat, zum konzentrierten Ausdruck der Ware oder des Geschäftsbetriebes werden, ohne diese deshalb sichtbar werden zu lassen.

Zwischen der großflächigen Verglasung, die eine direkte Verbindung des Geschäfts mit der Straße herstellt, und der fensterlosen Fassade mit unauffälligen Eingängen, liegt ein breiter Spielraum architektonischer Lösungen. In jedem Fall hängt die Wahl eines bestimmten Fassadentyps mehr oder weniger von der Gegenüberstellung folgender Kriterien ab:
— Typ des Geschäfts und der Verkaufsware;
— Verkaufspolitik: Massenkundschaft, Luxuskundschaft, Snob-Kundschaft usw.;
— Art der Verkaufsware, ihr Aussehen und ihre Qualität;
— Konkurrenz;
— Architektonische Notwendigkeiten: Integration der Fassade in das Gebäude, in dem sich das Geschäft befindet (Gebäude unter Denkmalschutz oder mit sehr charakteristischer Architektur), sowie Integration in die bauliche Umgebung.

Obwohl diese Kriterien ein zusammenhängendes Ganzes bilden, sollen sie einzeln analysiert werden, um nützliche Erkenntnisse zu gewinnen.

*Der Typ des Geschäfts und der Verkaufsware*
Ein Schmuckstück wird nicht in der gleichen Weise ausgestellt wie ein Koffer oder ein Motorrad. Ist schon der Interessentenkreis für diese Waren verschieden, so kommt noch dazu, daß jede dieser Waren spezifische Dimensionen besitzt, die den Charakter der Fassade und die spezielle Beschaffenheit der Schaufenster mehr oder weniger zwingend bestimmen. Es bieten sich zwei Lösungen an:
— Die vollständige Verglasung:
Diese Lösung hat den Vorzug einer großen Auslagefläche, benötigt jedoch, je nach dem Ausmaß der ausgestellten Gegenstände, eine Unterteilung, die den Ausstellungsmodulen im Inneren ange-

trade in question and a logical scheme of circulation for customers and staff.

Shopfitting, whether in a department store or in a boutique, is a matter for the expert. Even before the charm of the interior comes into play, however, it is logical, indeed essential, that the passer-by, i.e. the potential customer, should be persuaded to step inside. The most obvious means of persuasion is of course window-dressing, though this is not and need not always be the case. Architecturally the shop front can have the quality of a sign or an announcement, for example; it can constitute a synthesis of the product or business concerned without overtly displaying either.

The range of possible architectural solutions is enormous—from the plate-glass wall that brings the shop into direct contact with the street to the virtually blind front pierced by a few discreet apertures. In any event the choice of front type will depend to a greater or lesser extent upon a combination of the following factors:
— the type of business conducted and product sold;
— the shop's commercial policy: mass clientele, luxury or snob trade, etc.;
— the nature, appearance, and quality of the product sold;
— the competition;
— architectural constraints, i.e. the shop's relationship to the building it occupies—above all in the case of scheduled or particularly characteristic buildings, for example—and to its architectural environment.

It is of course the combination that counts, but let us for the purposes of analysis look at each of these factors in turn.

*The type of business conducted and product sold*
A piece of jewellery is not going to be displayed in the same way as a suitcase or a motorcycle. Not only does each product have a different type of clientele; it also has its own particular scale, which will to a greater or lesser extent determine the character of the shop front and of the display windows. There are two possible solutions:
— Glazing the whole front:
This offers a large display area but, depending on the size of the objects displayed, calls for some subdivision as regards the display units within. This can be done when the shop is being fitted out and decorated.
— Subdivision within the architectural conception of the front:

Une chaîne de magasin peut, par ce procédé, offrir une image de marque définie à partir d'études précises sur le produit vendu.

*La politique commerciale*
Elle est déterminée par la situation géographique nationale et locale (ville, quartier, rue). En effet, le même type de commerce se valorisera différemment selon sa situation dans un secteur populaire ou résidentiel, snob ou conformiste.
Le style de la clientèle inspirera ainsi une tendance dans le choix des formes et des matériaux. Ceux-ci peuvent intriguer, amuser, mais ils ne doivent jamais créer un malaise pour la clientèle locale: la débauche de marbre et d'acier peut séduire ici et intimider là.

*La nature du produit vendu, son aspect, sa qualité*
Ces trois composants entrent aussi largement en ligne de compte. A titre d'exemple, un produit comestible, même de luxe, ne nécessite pas « forcément » le même environnement qu'un objet décoratif.
Si, en architecture pure, les données d'un « programme » sont assez claires, ici, elles sont très suggestives et fluctuantes. Un bon commerçant, un architecte ou un installateur avisé saura trouver la juste mesure.

*La concurrence*
La clientèle aime la diversité, elle est attirée par la nouveauté. La rue traditionnelle (les centres commerciaux sont conçus différemment) est triste et peu attrayante si les magasins sont uniformes. Lorsqu'un concurrent direct connaît un certain succès commercial, il est plus habile de s'en différencier que de le copier. Une structure générale et une composition nouvelles, des couleurs et des matériaux mis en œuvre d'une autre manière auront un impact réel sur le public en aiguisant sa curiosité.

*Les obligations architecturales*
Une façade de magasin doit-elle se conformer au style architectural de la maison dans laquelle elle s'inscrit ou du quartier environnant? Lorsque les règlements locaux ne sont pas précis et impératifs, le créateur dispose d'une plus grande liberté. Il peut exalter les traits caractéristiques de l'architecture existante, sans pour cela les démarquer. Il peut aussi affirmer sa composition par une audace ne tenant compte que de l'impact visuel. Dans cette optique, il est prudent de connaître les limites qui séparent l'originalité du mauvais goût: à ce titre, une accumulation de matériaux et de couleurs est déjà inquiétante.

paßt ist, die ihrerseits bei der Einrichtung und Dekoration des Geschäfts installiert werden können.
— Die Unterteilung als architektonisches Gestaltungsprinzip der Fassade:
Diese — gestalterisch anspruchsvollere — Lösung bringt Ton und Charakter des Geschäfts unverwechselbar zum Ausdruck. Sie weckt die Aufmerksamkeit und Neugier des Passanten in gleicher Weise wie eine Plastik, ein modernes Flachrelief, und lenkt sie dann auf Auslagen, die vollkommen auf die Ware abgestimmt sind.
Eine Ladenkette kann durch diese Methode ein bestimmtes Image erhalten, das auf präzise Marktstudien über die Verkaufsware aufgebaut ist.

*Die Verkaufspolitik*
Sie hängt von der Lage des Geschäfts im nationalen und regionalen Raum ab (Stadt, Viertel, Straße). Das gleiche Geschäft kommt je nach seiner Lage in einem vornehmen oder einfachen Viertel, einer snobistischen oder konformistischen Gegend verschieden an.
Der Stil der Kundschaft legt daher eine bestimmte Ausrichtung in der Wahl von Form und Material nahe. Diese Mittel können auffallend oder unkonventionell sein, doch dürfen sie bei der einheimischen Kundschaft niemals ein Gefühl des Unbehagens auslösen: Der verschwenderische Umgang mit Marmor und Stahl kann hier anziehend und dort einschüchternd wirken.

*Die Art der Verkaufsware, ihr Aussehen, ihre Qualität*
Diese drei Komponenten nehmen ebenso einen breiten Raum in den Überlegungen ein. Zum Beispiel braucht ein eßbares Produkt, selbst der Luxusqualität, nicht « zwangsläufig » die gleiche Umgebung wie ein Dekorationsgegenstand.
Wenn die Gegebenheiten eines « Programms » im Bereich der reinen Architektur ziemlich klar und eindeutig sind, so unterliegen sie hier sehr suggestiven und wechselnden Anforderungen. Ein guter Geschäftsmann, ein Architekt oder ein geschickter Installateur findet hier das richtige Mittelmaß.

*Die Konkurrenz*
Die Kundschaft schätzt die Verschiedenartigkeit, das Neue zieht sie an. Die traditionelle Einkaufsstraße (Ladenzentren sind anders angelegt) wirkt trist und wenig verlockend, wenn die Geschäfte alle gleich sind. Hat ein direkter Konkurrent geschäftlichen Erfolg, ist es ratsamer, sich etwas vollkommen anderes einfallen zu lassen statt ihn nachzuahmen. Eine neue Gesamtstruktur und Komposition, Farben und Material in neuartiger Zu-

This is the bolder solution, announcing the tone and character of the business in a way that cannot be ignored. It excites and intrigues the passer-by much as a sculpture or a modern bas-relief would, drawing his attention to a display that can then be perfectly adapted to the product concerned.
In this way a chain of shops can project a brand image based on detailed market research.

*Commercial policy*
This will depend on the shop's geographical position, both national and local (town, district, street). In fact the same type of business will differ according to whether it is situated in a working-class area, in a residential suburb, or in a posh quarter.
The nature of the clientele will tend to dictate the choice of shapes and materials. These may be intriguing, they may be amusing, but they must never make the local clientele feel ill at ease. A marble and steel extravaganza, while attracting one kind of clientele, will intimidate another.

*The nature, appearance, and quality of the product sold*
All three factors are of equal importance. For example a particular foodstuff, even if it is a luxury article, will not necessarily call for the same setting as a decorative object.
In pure architecture the data of a 'programme' are generally pretty clear-cut; here they are extremely fluid and allusive. A good businessman, an architect, and a shopfitter who knows what he is doing will be able to get the proportions right.

*The competition*
The purchasing public likes variety and is attracted by everything new. The traditional street (shopping centres are differently conceived) presents a dismal, unattractive prospect if all the shops look the same. When a direct competitor hits a winning streak it is smarter to do something different than to copy what he has done. A new overall structure and layout plus a different use of colours and materials will have a real impact on the public by whetting its curiosity.

*Architectural constraints*
Ought a shop front to conform to the architecture of the building the shop occupies and the quarter in which it is situated? In the absence of detailed and binding local by-laws on this point the designer has a greater measure of freedom. He can heighten the distinctive features of the existing architecture without necessarily impairing their identity, or he can boldly assert his composition in

Dans de nombreux pays où l'architecture de certains quartiers est préservée, les pouvoirs publics obligent les commerçants renouvelant la structure de leur magasin à intégrer celle-ci le plus discrètement possible aux constructions existantes. Ainsi, les arcades anciennes, les ouvertures cernées de pierres ou de briques rejointoyées avec soin serviront de cadre à de vastes glaces claires ou fumées au travers desquelles le regard découvrira parfois une belle confrontation de l'architecture ancienne avec des éléments structurels et des meubles résolument contemporains. L'Italie semble pour le moment avoir le mieux assimilé ce principe. Peut-être pourrait-on trouver d'autres formules intéressantes, mais il faut admettre que cette solution coupe court à des outrances discutables.

## LES MOYENS

### La conception générale de la façade

Une fois que le « parti » est déterminé, que toutes les orientations possibles ont été étudiées, confrontées, et que les limites de la recherche sont précises, la conception entre dans sa phase principale.

Lorsqu'une façade de magasin est plaquée sur un volume intérieur existant, ancien ou aménagé très simplement et économiquement, la grande glace sol-plafond s'avère être la formule la plus franche, la mieux adaptée.

Dans le cas où la restructuration du local est totale, la physionomie extérieure gagnera à être conçue selon la même démarche intellectuelle et dans le même élan créatif qui ont abouti au choix des volumes intérieurs. Le passage de la rue vers l'intérieur doit être évident, harmonieux. Quand un visiteur pousse la porte d'un magasin, il apprécie d'y trouver l'ambiance et le climat esthétique que la façade lui a promis.

Les proportions du gros œuvre sont en partie déterminantes, mais les impératifs techniques orienteront également l'allure de la future façade. Parmi eux, la présence de piliers est la plus contraignante, car il n'est pas toujours possible de les supprimer ou d'engager les travaux pour le faire (reprise en sous-œuvre des murs latéraux, passage de filets métalliques). Selon que ces piliers existent ou non, la distribution intérieur-extérieur, et en particulier la disposition des accès, se concevra différemment. Que ce soit au centre

sammenstellung und Anwendung, sprechen das Publikum direkt an, indem sie seine Neugier wekken.

### Die architektonischen Notwendigkeiten
Muß sich die Fassade eines Geschäfts dem architektonischen Stil des Hauses oder des Viertels, in dem es liegt, anpassen? Wenn keine genauen und verbindlichen Bestimmungen der lokalen Behörden vorliegen, hat der Architekt einen größeren gestalterischen Spielraum. Er kann die charakteristischen Züge der vorhandenen Architektur betonen, ohne sie deswegen klischeehaft nachzuahmen. Eine andere Möglichkeit ist die völlig freie Fassadengestaltung, die nur auf die optische Wirkung ausgerichtet ist. Hier kommt es darauf an, die Grenze zwischen Originalität und Geschmacksverirrung streng zu wahren. In dieser Hinsicht ist eine Vielzahl von Material und Farbe bereits gefährlich.
In vielen Ländern bestehen für bestimmte Viertel, deren Architektur unter Denkmalschutz steht, behördliche Bestimmungen beim Umbau von Geschäftsräumen, die eine möglichst unauffällige Eingliederung der Fassade in die vorhandenen Bauten vorschreiben. So werden alte Arkaden, Maueröffnungen mit sorgfältig verfugter Natur- oder Backsteineinfassung zum Rahmen für große, durchsichtige oder dunkel gefärbte Schaufenster, durch die hindurch sich dem Blick manchmal eine gelungene Gegenüberstellung der alten Architektur mit modernen Strukturelementen und einer modernen Einrichtung offenbart. Dieses Prinzip scheint in Italien im Augenblick am besten verwirklicht zu werden. Es ließen sich vielleicht auch andere interessante Möglichkeiten finden, doch muß eingeräumt werden, daß diese Lösung überspitzte Kompositionen, die Ansichtssache sind, von vornherein unterbindet.

## TECHNISCHE UND GESTALTERISCHE MITTEL

### Der Entwurf der Fassade

Wenn die grundsätzliche Entscheidung einmal gefallen ist, alle Möglichkeiten durchdacht und die Grenzen der Planung genau abgesteckt worden sind, tritt der Entwurf in seine zentrale Phase.
Wird eine Geschäftsfassade auf einen bereits vor-

a way that takes account of nothing but visual impact. The latter solution should not be embarked upon without a clear idea of exactly where originality ends and bad taste begins. Quantities of different materials and colours, for example, are already cause for alarm.
In many countries where the architecture of particular quarters is scheduled for preservation the public authorities make tradesmen wishing to remodel their shops do so in such a way as to make them fit as discreetly as possible into the architectural environment. Arches, for example, or apertures with stone or nicely repointed brickwork surrounds will be the ideal setting for vast panes of clear or frosted glass through which the eye may occasionally glimpse splendid juxtapositions of period architecture and uncompromisingly modern structural elements and furnishings. At the moment Italy appears to have learned this lesson best.
Possibly other interesting formulas might be found, but this solution certainly does obviate the controversial and the outrageous.

## METHODS

### Designing a shop front

Once all avenues of research have been exhausted, all the possible solutions compared, and a particular 'line' decided on, the main design stage begins.
When a shop front is being added to an existing interior, to old premises or premises that have been very simply and economically converted, the most honest and the most suitable solution is always the full-length, floor-to-ceiling window.
In the case of premises that are being completely rebuilt, the shop's 'face' will gain by being designed within the same intellectual context and on the basis of the same creative impulse as have governed the choice of volumes in the interior. The transition from street to shop must be smooth and unambiguous. When a potential customer pushes open the door he wants to find the kind of ambiance and aesthetic climate that the shop front has led him to expect.
The proportions of the basic building are to some extent determinative, but the look of the future shop front will be influenced by other imperatives of a technical order. The most awkward of these is

de la façade, latéralement, en angle, en retrait, etc., chaque solution possède ses défauts, ses qualités, corrigées ou valorisées par le jeu des proportions de la structure générale. Deux variantes exigent une courte explication:

*Le sas ouvert*
Plus ou moins important, il abrite le passant et permet aux vitrines de se retourner latéralement, ce qui améliore la présentation de la marchandise (voir pp. 58-61).

*La galerie-hall*
La séparation entre l'intérieur et l'extérieur se trouve ici en retrait du mur extérieur de l'immeuble. La galerie ainsi créée offre des vitrines latérales et parfois des vitrines centrales (voir pp. 160, 161 et 163). La surface de présentation s'en trouve considérablement augmentée. Le passant est attiré vers l'intérieur. Dans ce cas, la véritable façade sur rue se réduit bien souvent à un habillage du bandeau frontal et des pilastres.
Cette formule commercialement intéressante n'est possible que lorsque la surface au sol est généreuse.

Autour de ces principes clefs — accès affleurant la façade, sas et galerie-hall —, peuvent s'articuler une infinité de compositions dont il serait vain de faire un inventaire. Voici par contre un survol des trois composants mobiles principaux de l'architecture d'une devanture. En toute logique, nous débuterons par:

La porte

Simple ou double, pleine ou vitrée, la porte doit se manœuvrer aisément et d'une façon évidente. La poignée, s'il en existe une, est grande, et ne doit pas offrir de forme agressive autant pour le regard que pour la main.
L'ouverture peut se faire automatiquement: le client chargé de paquets apprécie ce raffinement. Dans ce cas, deux formules sont proposées:
— Si le débattement des panneaux est traditionnel, deux passages sont indispensables, l'un consacré à l'entrée, l'autre à la sortie.
— Si les panneaux coulissent latéralement, un seul passage suffit.
Dans l'un et l'autre cas, la commande s'effectue soit par cellule photo-électrique située à l'intérieur et à l'extérieur entre 1,50 et 2 m avant le seuil, soit

handenen, alten oder sehr einfach angelegten Innenraum aufgesetzt, empfiehlt sich ein großes, in ganzer Höhe durchgehendes Schaufenster als die großzügigste, passendste Lösung.
Falls der Geschäftsraum von Grund auf neu gestaltet wird, ist es günstiger, wenn die Außenfassade nach denselben intellektuellen Prinzipien und mit demselben schöpferischen Elan entworfen wird, die für das Konzept der Innenräume bestimmend waren. Der Zugang von der Straße in das Innere muß gut sichtbar und flüssig angelegt sein. Beim Betreten eines Geschäfts empfindet es der Kunde als angenehm, wenn er dort die Atmosphäre und ästhetische Umgebung findet, die ihm die Fassade versprochen hat.
Die Proportionen des Gesamtgebäudes sind zum Teil bestimmend für die Gesaltung der Ladenfassade, doch wird ihr künftiges Aussehen ebenso von den technischen Notwendigkeiten beeinflußt. Darunter stellt das Vorhandensein von Stützpfeilern den zwingendsten Fall dar, da es nicht immer möglich ist, sie ganz zu entfernen oder sie in den Unterbau der Seitenwände miteinzubeziehen, der von Metallgittern durchzogen wird. Die Aufteilung von Innen- und Außenbereich und speziell die Anordnung der Zugänge gestaltet sich verschieden, je nachdem ob diese Pfeiler vorhanden sind oder nicht. Gleich ob der Eingang in der Mitte, an der Seite, an der Ecke oder hinter die Fassade zurückgesetzt liegt usw., jede Lösung hat ihre Nachteile und ihre Vorzüge, die durch das Proportionenspiel der Gesamtanlage ausgeglichen, beziehungsweise zur Geltung gebracht werden. Zwei Varianten bedürfen einer kurzen Erklärung:

*Der offene Vorraum*
Mehr oder minder geräumig, bietet er dem Passanten Schutz und Unterstand und ermöglicht zugleich eine seitliche Fortsetzung der Auslagen, wodurch eine bessere Ausstellung der Ware erreicht wird (siehe S. 58-61).

*Die Kombination von Halle und Galerie*
Die Trennungslinie zwischen Innen- und Außenbereich ist hier hinter die Außenwand des Gebäudes zurückgesetzt. Die so entstandene Galerie enthält Schaufenster an den Seiten und manchmal auch Vitrinenblöcke in der Mitte (siehe S. 160, 161 und 163). Die Ausstellungsfläche wird dadurch erheblich vergrößert und der Passant in das Innere gezogen. Bei dieser Lösung ist die eigentliche Straßenfassade oft nur auf eine Verkleidung der Frontplatte und der Stützpfeiler beschränkt.
Diese in kommerzieller Hinsicht interessante Lösung ist nur möglich, wenn sehr viel Fläche zur Verfügung steht.

the presence of pillars, because it is not always possible to get rid of them (i.e. by underpinning the side walls, using metal beams, etc.). The division between interior and exterior and in particular the position of the door or doors will be different if they have to take account of pillars than if they do not. Whether the doors are in the centre of the shop front, at the sides, on a corner, set back, or anywhere else, each solution has its advantages and its disadvantages, each of which will in turn be heightened or reduced by the overall play of proportions. Two variants call for special mention:

*The recessed entrance*
The resultant open vestibule, which can be of any width or depth, offers shelter to the passer-by and makes it possible to turn the display windows through an angle, improving their display effect (see pp. 58-61).

*The gallery*
Here the division between shop and exterior occurs some way back from the outside wall of the building, leaving a gallery that can accommodate display windows at the sides and even in the middle, thus considerably increasing the display surface (see pp. 160, 161 and 163). The passer-by finds himself drawn towards the interior of the shop. In this case the actual shop front on the street will often consist of no more than the facia or name plate and supporting pilasters. This is an advantageous solution commercially, but it is only possible with a large floor area.

Around these three main solutions—façade entrance, outside vestibule, and gallery—there is an infinite number of possible variants and it would be pointless to try and list them all. What we will do instead is take a quick look at the three principal moving architectural components of the shop front, starting, logically enough, with:

The door

Whether single- or double-leaved, solid or glazed, the door must be easy and uncomplicated to open. The handle, if any, should be large, and any aggressiveness of appearance or feel is to be avoided.
The door may be made to open automatically—a refinement that will be appreciated by customers with their arms full of purchases. Two solutions are possible here:

par pression au sol sur une plaque métallique située dans l'axe du passage et protégée par un revêtement souple, le plus souvent un tapis caoutchouté. Lorsque l'ouverture est automatique, le sas double paraît indispensable.

Les fermetures de protection

Afin de limiter les effractions possibles, ces fermetures obturent tout ou partie de la façade, particulièrement les parties vitrées, et sont utilisées durant les heures et les jours où le magasin n'est pas en activité.

*Le rideau métallique à lames pleines*
Lorsque le rideau est ouvert, ces lames, assez larges, se regroupent les unes derrière les autres sous un bandeau ou dans un caisson conçu à cet effet, placé sur le haut de la façade. Ce type de fermeture (un des plus anciens) est assez inesthétique; il se manœuvre avec difficulté et ne peut s'adapter qu'à des façades traditionnelles.

*Le rideau métallique enroulable*
Il nécessite aussi un caisson supérieur. Le plus ancien est en tôle ondulée, mais son aspect triste et sa manœuvre fatigante lui valent d'être abandonné au profit de rideaux plus légers, tout aussi solides, réalisés en lames d'acier articulées dont il existe de nombreux profils. Ces rideaux peuvent être peints ou conservés naturels, car ils sont généralement en acier galvanisé.
Comme il est illogique de choisir l'une de ces formules d'obturation totale si l'on désire que le magasin participe à l'animation de la rue (surtout la nuit), et que ses vitrines séduisent le promeneur, éventuel « acheteur du lendemain », il sera possible de retenir le *rideau-grille.* Il est réalisé en tube d'acier dont les ondulations constituent des mailles plus ou moins écartées. Ce rideau rend la façade plus élégante tout en permettant de voir l'intérieur du magasin. Tous ces rideaux peuvent se commander électriquement et se dérouler devant ou derrière les glaces, offrant ainsi au créateur une plus grande liberté dans la composition générale et particulièrement dans le choix de l'emplacement du caisson d'enroulement.

*La grille articulée dépliable*
Elle se replie latéralement dans des caissons ouvrants (voir p. 134). Dépliée, elle permet de voir

Um diese Grundprinzipien — Eingang in der Fluchtlinie der Fassade, offener Vorraum und galerieartige Eingangshalle — gruppieren sich unendlich viele Gestaltungsmöglichkeiten, auf deren Aufzählung verzichtet werden kann. Dafür soll hier ein knapper Überblick über die drei mobilen Hauptkomponenten in der Architektur einer Geschäftsfassade gegeben werden. Dabei wird nach der logischen Reihenfolge vorgegangen.

Die Tür

Ob ein- oder zweiflügelig, kompakt oder verglast, die Tür muß leicht und ohne Orientierungsschwierigkeit bewegt werden können. Der Türgriff, wenn vorhanden, soll groß sein, und darf keine aggressive Form aufweisen, weder für die Hand noch im Aussehen.
Die Tür kann sich auch automatisch öffnen: Der mit Paketen beladene Kunde wird diesen Komfort als angenehm empfinden. In diesem Fall gibt es zwei Möglichkeiten:
— Wenn die Türflügel in konventioneller Weise auf- und zuschwingen, sind zwei Passagen unerläßlich, eine als Eingang, die andere als Ausgang.
— Wenn die Türflügel nach der Seite aufgehen, genügt eine einzige Passage.
In beiden Fällen erfolgt die automatische Betätigung entweder durch photoelektrische Zellen, die innen und außen in einem Abstand von 1,50 bis 2 Meter zur Türschwelle eingebaut sind, oder durch Druck auf eine in den Boden eingelassene Metallplatte, die quer zur Passage verläuft und mit einem schmiegsamen Belag, zumeist einer Gummimatte, abgedeckt ist. Bei automatischer Türöffnung scheint eine doppelte Türpassage unentbehrlich.

Schutzvorrichtungen

Um die Gefahr von Einbrüchen in Grenzen zu halten, wird die Fassade ganz oder teilweise, insbesondere an den verglasten Flächen, mit Schutzvorrichtungen abgedeckt, die ausserhalb der Geschäftszeiten in Betrieb genommen werden.

*Der Vorhang aus kompakten Metallplatten*
Wenn der Vorhang offen ist, liegen die ziemlich breiten Platten hintereinander geklappt unter einer Blende oder in einem speziell dafür konstruierten, oben an der Fassade angebrachten Kasten. Dieser Typ der Schutzvorrichtung (einer der ältesten) ist

— If the leaves of the door open in the traditional manner, two doors are essential—an entrance and an exit.
— In the case of sliding leaves, a single door is sufficient.
In both cases the door will be controlled either by photo-electric cells inside and out at a distance of between one and a half and two metres from the threshold or by pressure on a metal platform situated in the axis of the doorway and covered with some soft covering, usually rubber matting. Automatic doors in principle call for an 'air-lock' system.

Security shutters

In order to prevent burglaries the whole or part of the shop front—particularly of course the glazed portions—can be shuttered off during the night and on days when the shop is closed. There are three main kinds of security shutter:

*The solid-leaf metal shutter*
In the open position the leaves, which are fairly broad, fit one behind the other up behind the facia or in a special housing fitted at the top of the shop front. This type of shutter—one of the oldest—is not particularly attractive; moreover it is awkward to open and close and can only be fitted to the traditional shop front.

*The roll-up metal shutter*
This too requires a housing at the top of the shop front. The oldest type is of corrugated iron. Depressing in appearance and tiring to operate, it has been abandoned in favour of lighter though equally strong types of shutter made of hinged steel slats of various shapes. They can be either painted or left as they are, which is generally galvanized.
Since it makes no sense to close off one's shop entirely if one wants it to be part of the life of the street (especially at night) and since the passer-by who sees and is attracted by a shop window today may be a customer tomorrow, another possibility is the *grille-type shutter.* This is made of tubular steel forming a more or less wide mesh. Such a shutter heightens the elegance of the shop front while still enabling people to see inside. All these types of shutter can be controlled electrically and can come down in front of or behind the windows, thus leaving the designer considerable freedom in the matter of overall composition and particularly in his choice of where to place the shutter housing.

l'intérieur du magasin, mais son emploi ne reste valable que pour les très petites façades, car, dans le cas contraire, la mise en place lors de la fermeture est fastidieuse. En outre, l'entretien est assez long et délicat.

A titre d'information complémentaire, il est aussi envisageable pour clore un magasin d'installer un rideau constitué de lames de bois ou de plastique. Ces rideaux obturent totalement, ce qui peut être commercialement néfaste (voir plus haut) et leur efficacité contre les effractions est moins évidente que celle des rideaux métalliques.
Ces diverses fermetures sont industrialisées, mais le créateur confronté à ce problème trouvera probablement d'autres solutions que l'installateur pourra réaliser spécialement. Fort heureusement pour l'originalité de certaines recherches, tous les commerçants ne jugent pas indispensable de fermer ainsi leur magasin. En effet, de nouvelles glaces (armées discrètement ou non) offrent une résistance exceptionnelle aux chocs, et leur emploi est accepté par les compagnies d'assurances.

Les stores

Afin d'assurer une protection contre le soleil ou la pluie, le store s'avère souvent très appréciable. Il est possible, dans de nombreux cas, d'installer un store sur une façade existante au prix de quelques transformations, mais lors d'une installation complète, mieux vaut le prévoir tout de suite, car son intégration sera plus élaborée. Deux modèles ont fait leur preuve:

*Le store-banne*
Une fois déplié, il peut s'étendre très en avant de la façade; selon l'importance de cette dernière et sa hauteur, l'installateur compétent saura lui donner la pente nécessaire pour éviter les poches d'eau en cas de pluie. Son déploiement est assuré par des bras métalliques articulés.

*Le store-corbeille*
Son avancée est toujours plus réduite que celle du store-banne et prend l'aspect d'une marquise. Il est constitué d'une série d'arceaux métalliques sur lesquels est tendu le tissu. Ces arceaux se retournent latéralement et se rejoignent en un point servant de pivot (voir pp. 104-105). Une fois replié, ce type de store ne nécessite pas un logement aussi important que l'autre modèle. Il peut même rester visible, ce qui adoucit l'architecture de la façade.

ästhetisch wenig ansprechend; er läßt sich nur schwer bewegen und ist nur für konventionelle Fassaden verwendbar.

*Der ausrollbare Metallvorhang*
Bei diesem Typ muß der Kasten oben liegen. Das älteste Modell besteht aus Wellblech, von dem man jedoch auf Grund des unschönen Anblicks und der unhandlichen Bedienung abgekommen ist. Man verwendet jetzt leichtere, doch ebenso stabile Modelle aus beweglichen Stahllamellen, die in zahlreichen Profilstärken vorliegen. Diese Schutzvorrichtungen können gestrichen oder naturbelassen werden, da sie im allgemeinen aus verzinktem Stahl bestehen.
Eine dieser Schutzvorrichtungen zu wählen, die eine vollkommene Abdeckung erzielen, ist wenig sinnvoll, wenn das Geschäft am Leben in den Straßen, insbesondere nachts, teilnehmen soll und die Schaufenster für den Spaziergänger und potentiellen « Käufer von morgen » einen Anreiz bieten sollen. Hier bietet sich die Lösung des *Schutzgitters* an. Es besteht aus Stahlrohr, dessen wellenförmige Biegungen eine weit- oder engmaschige Struktur bilden. Diese Schutzvorrichtung gibt der Fassade ein eleganteres Gesicht und ermöglicht gleichzeitig den Einblick in das Innere des Geschäfts. Alle derartigen Vorrichtungen können elektrisch bedient und vor oder hinter den Schaufensterscheiben ausgerollt werden, so daß dem Gestalter ein größerer Spielraum in der Gesamtkomposition und insbesondere bei der Wahl des Standorts für den Rollkasten bleibt.

*Das ausklappbare Schutzgitter*
Das Gitter wird in seitlich liegende Kästen zurückgeklappt (siehe S. 134). In geschlossenem Zustand hält es den Blick auf das Ladeninnere frei, doch empfiehlt sich diese Vorrichtung nur für sehr kleine Fassaden, da ihre jeweilige Anbringung im entgegengesetzten Fall ziemlich umständlich ist. Auch ist die Wartung ziemlich zeitraubend und anspruchsvoll.

Der Vollständigkeit halber sei noch auf die Möglichkeit hingewiesen, den Laden mit einer Jalousie aus Holz- oder Plastiklamellen zu schließen. Diese Vorrichtungen decken die Anlage allerdings vollständig ab, was sich in geschäftlicher Hinsicht ungünstig auswirken kann (siehe oben), und ihre Wirksamkeit gegen Einbrüche ist weniger groß als die der Schutzvorrichtungen aus Metall.
Diese Typen von Schutzvorrichtungen sind als Serienprodukte im Handel, doch bleibt dem mit diesem Problem konfrontierten Architekten die Möglichkeit, vom Installateur Spezialausführungen anfertigen zu lassen. Zum Glück halten nicht alle

*The folding hinged grille*
This folds sideways into lateral boxes (see p. 134). When closed it still allows a view of the interior, but it is only suitable for very small shop fronts. In the case of a large shop front this type of shutter is laborious to operate. It is also tricky and time-consuming to maintain.

For the sake of completeness we might also point out that there are shop shutters made of wooden or plastic slats. These completely obscure the interior, which may be bad for business (see above), and they are of course less effective against burglars than are metal shutters.
All these types of shutter are produced industrially, but the designer tackling this problem will probably find other solutions that can be 'made to measure' by the shopfitter. Fortunately for the originality of certain avenues of research in this field, not all shopkeepers consider it necessary to seal their premises in this way. And indeed there are new types of highly shock-resistant glass (some with discreet reinforcement) that insurance companies will accept for shop-front use.

Blinds

In order to provide protection against sun and rain, it is often a very good idea to have a blind. In many cases this can be fitted to an existing shop front with only a few modifications, but when a shop is being built from scratch it is better to get the blind in at the planning stage, where it can be incorporated in a more sophisticated manner. Two patterns have stood the test of time:

*The awning*
In the open position this can extend a long way out from the shop front, and depending on the size and height of the latter the competent shopfitter will give it the right degree of tilt in order to prevent pockets of water from forming. The awning type of blind folds in and out on hinged metal arms.

*The basket blind*
Never projecting as far as the flat awning, the basket blind gives more the impression of a canopy. It consists of a series of metal arcs over which the material is stretched. The arcs continue in lateral arms that come together at a single pivot (see pp. 104-5). When folded this type of blind does not require so large a housing as the awning type. It can even be left visible, which will have the effect of softening the lines of the shop front.

Ces deux types de store peuvent être commandés manuellement ou électriquement.

Les tissus proposés sont assez nombreux: toiles de coton, de lin, fibres synthétiques, mélanges divers, etc. Ces tissus reçoivent tous un traitement imperméabilisant et stabilisateur des couleurs. Le choix de la qualité se fera aisément. Il n'en est pas de même avec celui des coloris et des dessins: mieux vaut prendre garde aux fleurs et aux ramages. Le store doit esthétiquement confirmer le caractère de la devanture; il devra être choisi en accord avec le créateur qui saura trancher entre le charme et la mièvrerie.

## L'éclairage

Une façade si réussie soit-elle, aux vitrines très éclairées, ne peut se passer, la nuit venue, d'une mise en valeur qui la singularisera aux yeux des promeneurs, des badauds, des acheteurs. L'enseigne, le sigle lumineux (voir p. 176) sont des signaux indispensables, mais l'éclairage général ou partiel de l'extérieur possède beaucoup de séduction. Cet éclairage est délicat, puisque les sources lumineuses ne peuvent jamais (ou presque) se trouver très en avant du magasin. Chaque création de devanture inspire une formule qui lui est propre. Nous dégagerons tout de même quelques moyens généralement utilisés et qui assurent des résultats satisfaisants.

### L'éclairage d'ambiance
Il est obtenu par des spots diffusants, directionnels, flashes, fixés soit à l'extrémité, soit au long de supports horizontaux ou verticaux, nettement en avancée par rapport à la façade (voir pp. 72, 74 et 75). Ces appareils exposés aux intempéries doivent présenter les garanties de sécurité imposées.

### L'éclairage frisant
Il est constitué de lampes incandescentes, fluorescentes, ou de tubes néon (parfois un mélange des trois). Ces sources lumineuses sont dissimulées dans les décrochements de la construction (voir pp. 30-33). Elles laissent dans l'ombre certains reliefs en mettant l'accent sur d'autres.

### L'éclairage « signal »
Il est assuré par un ceinturage de diverses surfaces ou volumes au moyen de tubes néon ou d'alignement de lampes incandescentes. Des surfaces entières peuvent être également équipées de ces sources lumineuses. Dans ce cas, il faut prendre

Geschäftsleute einen derartigen Verschluß ihres Ladens für erforderlich. Neuentwickelte Schaufensterscheiben (mit oder ohne unauffälliger Armierung) besitzen eine außergewöhnliche Widerstandsfähigkeit gegen Stöße und werden daher von den Versicherungsgesellschaften akzeptiert.

## Markisen

Eine Markise erweist sich oft als sehr vorteilhaft zum Schutz gegen Sonne und Regen. In zahlreichen Fällen ist es möglich, an einer vorhandenen Fassade mit wenigen Änderungen nachträglich eine Markise anzubringen; bei einer vollständigen Neugestaltung empfiehlt es sich jedoch, die Markise von vornherein in die Planung miteinzubeziehen, da ihre Integration in die Gesamtkonzeption durchdachter wirkt. Zwei Modelle haben sich bewährt:

### Die Rollmarkise
Ausgerollt deckt sie eine große Fläche vor der Fassade ab. Je nach Ausmaß und Höhe der Fassade muß die entsprechende Neigung für den Ablauf des Regenwassers berechnet werden, damit sich kein Wasser auf der Markise sammelt. Die Aufspannung des Vordachs erfolgt durch bewegliche Metallarme.

### Der Baldachin
Seine Spannweite ist stets geringer als die der Rollmarkise. Er besteht aus einer Reihe von Metallrundbögen, über die der Stoff gespannt ist. Diese Bögen laufen seitlich an einem Punkt zusammen, der als Scharnier dient (siehe S. 104-105). Dieser Typ des Vordachs benötigt keine so stabile Lagerung wie das andere Modell. Das Dach kann sogar aufgespannt bleiben, wodurch die Architektur der Fassade aufgelockert wird.

Beide Typen können elektrisch oder von Hand bedient werden.

Die Stoffauswahl ist ziemlich groß: Baumwollstoffe, Segeltuch, Synthetics, verschiedene Mischgewebe usw. Jeder dieser Stoffe erhält eine chemische Behandlung, die Wasserundurchlässigkeit und Farbechtheit garantiert. Die Auswahl nach der Stoffqualität fällt leicht. Schwieriger ist die Entscheidung hinsichtlich der Farben und Muster; Vorsicht vor Blumen- und Rankenmustern! Das Vordach muß mit dem ästhetischen Konzept der Auslage übereinstimmen; bei seiner Auswahl sollte der betreffende Gestalter zu Rate gezogen werden,

Both types of blind can be controlled manually or electrically.

A number of materials suggest themselves: calico, canvas, synthetic fibres, various mixtures, etc. These materials will be waterproofed and treated to make the colours fast. The choice of quality will present no problems. Not so the choice of colour and pattern: flowers and floral patterns in general should be used with circumspection. The blind should provide aesthetic confirmation of the character of the shop front as a whole; it should be chosen in consultation with the designer, who will know the dividing-line between charm and affectation.

## Lighting

However successful a shop front and however brightly-lit its windows, it must have something extra to set it off at night and make it stand out in the eyes of the evening window-shopper and potential future customer. Signs and luminous insignia (see p. 176) are essential for catching the attention, but there is a lot to be said too for partially or wholly illuminating the outside. This is a tricky problem because the light sources can never (or hardly ever) be very far in front of the shop. Each shop-front design will suggest its own solution, but let us pick out two or three methods that are widely used and give satisfactory results.

### Ambient lighting
This is provided by diffused or beamed spots and flashlights fixed either to the ends of or along horizontal or vertical supports standing out some way from the shop front (see pp. 72, 74-5). Exposed to all weathers, such lamps must of course conform to strict safety requirements.

### Relief lighting
This is provided by ordinary or fluorescent bulbs or neon tubes, or sometimes by a combination of all three (see pp. 30-33). The light sources are concealed behind projecting portions of the shop front, highlighting certain features of the architecture and leaving others in shadow.

### Sign lighting
This is obtained by enclosing various areas or volumes by means of neon tubes or rows of bulbs, or covering whole surfaces with light sources. In the latter case care must be taken not to spoil the appearance of the shop front by daylight.
Finally certain portions of the front can be treated

garde à ne pas détruire la physionomie du magasin lorsqu'il est vu en plein jour.

Enfin, certaines parois de la façade, traitées en matériau diffusant (perspex, glace dépolie), peuvent, la nuit venue, s'éclairer selon des intensités diverses.

Une marquise, un auvent, sont des supports parfaits pour installer plusieurs types d'éclairage. Ils permettent en particulier de diffuser une lumière générale intense ou douce à la base de la façade, solution convenant aux commerçants ayant une vente extérieure.

Les trois types d'éclairage décrits peuvent être jumelés, être colorés, ou alternatifs grâce à une minuterie programmée. Toutefois, il ne faut jamais perdre de vue que l'éclairage primordial est celui de la vitrine et que la lumière environnante doit être étudiée avec soin afin d'éviter la vulgarité.

## Les matériaux

Quels que soient le lieu, l'importance, les proportions et la finalité commerciale d'un magasin, la construction de sa façade implique l'utilisation de plusieurs matériaux devant se compléter au mieux. Voici un panorama schématique des principaux, car une telle énumération ne peut se prétendre exhaustive, trop de nouveautés apparaissant chaque jour sur le marché.

### La glace, les produits verriers
Ils ont profondément marqué le visage de la devanture contemporaine, car la possibilité de couler des glaces de grandes dimensions a bousculé les techniques anciennes de subdivision des parties vitrées. Au lendemain de la Seconde Guerre mondiale, l'utilisation de ce matériau connut une grande vogue. Les recherches actuelles ont assimilé cette outrance parfois injustifiable et s'orientent maintenant vers des solutions inverses. La glace transparente destinée aux vitrines est proposée en plusieurs épaisseurs; elle peut être armée de longs fils métalliques parallèles, teintée, découpée selon les gabarits nécessaires et galbée à la demande. Elle se met en place soit dans un profilé noyé dans le gros œuvre, soit dans une huisserie de métal, plastique, ou bois.
Avec les autres produits verriers tels que les verres armés et profilés (translucides uniquement), les briques, les pavés de verre, les dalles de couleur, il est possible de construire des murs et des parois qui laissent filtrer la lumière d'où qu'elle vienne.
Enfin, les glaces émaillées, aux nombreuses couleurs, et les glaces argentées complètent cette palette déjà généreuse.

der sicher zwischen Effekt und Übertreibung zu unterscheiden weiß.

## Die Beleuchtung

Auch die gelungenste Geschäftsfassade mit hell erleuchteten Schaufenstern braucht nachts noch ein zusätzliches Merkmal, das sie in den Augen der Spaziergänger, Bummler und potentiellen Käufer von den anderen unterscheidet. Das Firmenschild, das Firmenzeichen in Leuchtschrift (siehe S. 176) sind unerläßliche Signale, doch besitzt die allgemeine oder partielle Beleuchtung des Außenbereichs darüber hinaus große Anziehungskraft. Diese Beleuchtung ist nicht einfach zu installieren, da die Beleuchtungskörper niemals (oder fast niemals) sehr weit vor der Fassadenfront angebracht werden können. Jede Schaufensterkomposition hat ihre spezifische Lösung. Wir greifen dennoch einige allgemein gebräuchliche Mittel heraus, die befriedigende Ergebnisse erzielen.

### Die allgemeine Beleuchtung
Man verwendet zu diesem Zweck lichtstreuende Spots, Punktstrahler oder Scheinwerfer, die entweder am seitlichen Ende der Fassade oder entlang den waagerechten oder senkrechten Stützelementen montiert werden, und zwar deutlich vor der Fassadenfront (siehe S. 72, 74 und 75). Da diese Beleuchtungskörper der Witterung ausgesetzt sind, müssen sie die erforderlichen Sicherheitsbestimmungen erfüllen.

### Die indirekte Beleuchtung
Sie besteht aus konventionellen Glühbirnen, Neon- oder Leuchtstoffröhren, manchmal auch aus einer Mischung aller drei Beleuchtungstypen. Diese Lichtquellen werden unsichtbar hinter Abstufungen und Vorsprüngen der Fassadenkonstruktion angebracht (siehe S. 30-33). Bestimmte Partien treten dadurch plastisch hervor, während andere im Dunkel bleiben.

### Die « Signalbeleuchtung »
Sie erscheint als Einfassung verschiedener Flächen oder Körper mit Neonröhren oder aneinandergereihten Glühbirnen. Auch können ganze Flächenpartien mit solchen Lichtquellen bestückt werden. In diesem Fall ist allerdings darauf zu achten, daß die Physiognomie der Geschäftsfassade bei Tag nicht zerstört wird.
Ferner können bestimmte, in lichtstreuendem Material (Perspex, Milchglas) ausgeführte Fassadenflächen bei Nacht in verschiedenen Lichtstärken erleuchtet werden.

in some light-diffusing material (perspex or frosted glass) and illuminated at night with varying degrees of intensity.

A canopy or solid awning makes the perfect support for a number of types of lighting. In particular it makes it possible to throw a general light, whether bright or soft, on the lower part of the shop front, which is a useful solution for shopkeepers who do business outside.
These three types of lighting can be used in combination, they can be coloured, and they can be made to alternate by means of programmed automatic switches. The thing to be borne constantly in mind is that what matters most is the lighting of the window; the ambient lighting must be very carefully planned if it is to avoid the pitfall of vulgarity.

## Materials

Whatever the situation, size, proportions, and commercial purpose of a shop, the construction of the front is going to involve a number of materials that must set one another off to their best advantage. We cannot hope to list them all because there are too many new products appearing on the market daily, but let us have a brief look at the principal ones.

### Glass and glass products
These have profoundly influenced the appearance of the modern shop front since the possibility of drawing very large sheets of glass swept away all the old techniques of subdivision into panes. There was a tremendous increase in the use of glass after the Second World War. Modern ideas have now assimilated what was at times an unjustifiable exaggeration in this respect and are tending towards the opposite type of solution. The transparent plate glass designed for display windows comes in several thicknesses; it can also be reinforced by means of parallel lengths of wire, tinted, cut to any shape, and curved to order. It can be fitted either in a metal channel sunk in the masonry or in a metal, plastic, or wooden frame.
With other glass products such as reinforced and frosted (merely translucent) glass, glass bricks, floor blocks, and coloured tiles it is possible to build walls and other partitions that let the light through.
Finally, to add to this already generous assortment, there are enamelled glasses and silvered glasses.

## Les produits métalliques

Ils sont nombreux et d'aspects divers:
Le *fer* ordinaire constitue souvent les armatures sur lesquelles vient se plaquer un habillage vissé, clipsé ou agrafé.
Le *métal chromé,* lumineux, peut constituer des huisseries, des tubes, des habillages plans ou courbes.
Le *cuivre* présente les mêmes possibilités, mais il doit recevoir une protection particulière pour ne pas s'oxyder. Sa mise en œuvre est artisanale.
La *tôle d'acier naturel,* très utilisée dans l'architecture actuelle, l'est également pour les façades de magasin. Elle est plane ou présente des reliefs obtenus par emboutissage. Elle se laque manuellement ou le plus souvent au four, et offre, en plus de toutes les couleurs imaginables, des finitions métallisées identiques à celles de l'automobile.
La *tôle d'acier inoxydable* présente les mêmes possibilités, mais elle reste évidemment naturelle. Des huisseries, des structures pleines sont réalisables en acier inoxydable.
L'*aluminium* est très utilisé actuellement. Il est léger, net, se travaille facilement et vite. Il est naturel ou anodisé (couleurs diverses). Employé pour la fabrication des huisseries, des tubes, l'aluminium constitue aussi le matériau d'une gamme importante de bardages aux profils multiples et combinables. Son prix de revient est relativement économique.

## Le bois

C'est un matériau « complet ». Il peut constituer à lui seul la structure et l'habillage d'une devanture grâce à ses multiples essences et à ses deux principales présentations: massif — débitable dans toutes les sections et épaisseurs (poteaux, planches, frises) —, ou plaqué (panneautages sur mesure ou standardisés).
Le bois se travaille aisément. Lorsqu'il n'est pas peint ou teinté (nombreux coloris), il faut le protéger de la pluie dès sa mise en place par l'application de vernis mats ou brillants.

## La pierre

Elle est utilisée dans bien des cas sous forme de parement dont l'épaisseur est très variable en fonction de sa nature même. La mise en place se fait par agrafage sur une structure en serrurerie ou par pose avec un mortier fin sur le gros œuvre. En plus des pierres traditionnelles — marbre, ardoise, granit —, l'industrie propose des plaques de pierres reconstituées ou de galets sciés.

## Les produits céramiques

Ce sont les briques, la terre cuite naturelle et vernissée, le grès cérame, les émaux. A part

---

Ein Vordach oder vorspringendes Element ist ideal für die Installation mehrerer Beleuchtungstypen. Sie ermöglichen insbesondere die Ausleuchtung der unteren Fassadenzone mit einem intensiven oder auch milden Licht; diese Lösung kommt vor allem für Geschäfte mit Außenverkauf in Frage.
Die drei Beleuchtungsarten können miteinander gekoppelt sein, farbiges Licht aufweisen oder, dank einer programmierten Uhr, alternativ geschaltet sein. Es darf jedoch niemals außer Acht gelassen werden, daß die Schaufensterbeleuchtung am wichtigsten ist und die Beleuchtung der Fassade sorgfältig abgestimmt sein muß, um eine grelle Wirkung zu vermeiden.

Verwendete Baustoffe

Unabhängig von Lage, Bedeutung, Proportionen und kommerzieller Bestimmung eines Geschäfts, werden beim Bau der Fassade verschiedene Materialien verwendet, die miteinander harmonieren müssen. Im Folgenden wird lediglich eine schematische Übersicht über die wichtigsten Gruppen gegeben; eine derartige Aufzählung kann nicht Anspruch auf Vollständigkeit erheben, da tagtäglich zu viele Neuheiten auf dem Markt erscheinen.

## Schaufensterglas, Glasbauprodukte

Diese Produkte haben das Gesicht der modernen Schaufensterauslagen grundlegend verändert, da die alten Techniken der Unterteilung verglaster Flächen durch die Möglichkeit, großflächige Glasscheiben im Gußverfahren herzustellen, verdrängt worden sind. Am Vorabend des Zweiten Weltkrieges erlebte die Verwendung dieses Baustoffes einen gewaltigen Boom. Die heutigen Untersuchungen haben diese manchmal bedenkliche Übertreibung auf das rechte Maß zurückgeführt und streben nunmehr entgegengesetzten Lösungen zu. Durchsichtiges Schaufensterglas wird in verschiedenen Stärken angeboten; es kann mit einer Armierung aus langen, parallelen Metallfäden ausgerüstet sein, kann eingefärbt, auf die erforderlichen Normen zugeschnitten sowie auf Wunsch rund sein. Die Verglasung ruht entweder in einem im Gebäude eingelassenen Profilblech oder in einem Rahmen aus Metall, Kunststoff oder Holz.
Mit anderen Glasprodukten wie armierten und ausgeformten (hier nur durchsichtigen) Glasscheiben, würfelartigen und rechteckigen Glasbausteinen, farbigen Glasfliesen, können Mauern und Zwischenwände erstellt werden, die das Licht von jeder Seite durchlassen.

---

## Metal products

These are many and various:
*Iron* often provides the frames onto which display fittings are bolted or otherwise fastened.
*Chromium-plated metal* can be used for door and window frames, tubes, and flat or curved display fittings.
*Copper* offers the same possibilities but needs to be treated to prevent it from oxydizing. Its use is a matter for the craftsman.
*Sheet steel,* much used in modern architecture, is extensively employed for shop fronts. It can be either flat or pressed into relief. It can be painted by hand, though it is usually fired, and offers, besides every colour imaginable, the kinds of metallic finish used for car bodies.
*Stainless sheet steel* offers the same possibilities but is of course left in the natural state. It can be used for both frames and solid structures.
*Aluminium* has become widely used. It is light, neat, and easy and quick to work. It can be left as it is or anodized (various colours). Used in the manufacture of frames and tubes, aluminium also provides a wide range of filling elements in a variety of profiles. In terms of cost it is relatively economical.

## Wood

Wood is an 'all-round' material. With its many qualities and in one or both of its two principal forms—solid, where it can be sawn to any section and width (beams, planks, strips), or ply, in standard or made-to-measure panels—it can provide the entire shop front by itself, structure and fittings. Wood is easy to work. If it is not painted or stained (wide choice of colours) it must be varnished (matt or gloss) as soon as it is put up to protect it from the rain.

## Stone

This is often used in the form of a facing, which by its very nature may be of almost any thickness. It is mounted on a metal framework or applied to the masonry by means of a fine mortar. In addition to the traditional stones—marble, slate, granite— slabs of composition stone and sawn cobles are also available.

## Ceramic products

These include brick, natural and glazed terracotta, stoneware, and glazes. Apart from a few types of brick (solid and honeycombed) they all take the form of facing.
Some of these products, e.g. stoneware and certain glazes, are produced industrially on a large scale and it is best to choose from the ranges offered by the manufacturers. Others, for example

quelques types de briques (pleines ou alvéolées), ils se présentent tous sous forme de parement. Certains de ces produits, comme le grès cérame et quelques émaux, sont largement industrialisés, et il est préférable de les choisir dans les gammes existantes proposées par les fabricants. Par contre, d'autres produits tels que la terre cuite sont produits de façon semi-artisanale, ce qui permet d'obtenir pour des cas très précis des éléments de claustra ou des modules, des plaques, des carreaux dimensionnés selon les besoins, présentant des motifs en relief, des couleurs et des finitions particulières.

Avec la brique traditionnelle utilisée dans l'architecture, il est possible de construire les parties aveugles d'une façade sans autre artifice qu'un jointoyage soigné. A noter que la brique se peint et se laque parfaitement.

### Les matières plastiques

Bien qu'elles ne soient pas toutes nouvelles, elles sont rarement utilisées au maximum de leurs propriétés.

Pour l'habillage des parties pleines, il existe des modules carrés, rectangulaires ou verticaux à relief, juxtaposables. Mais les techniques de pliage et de thermoformage offrent des possibilités multiples que seule la recherche pure, hors des sentiers battus, peut mettre en évidence. Ce matériau est coloré à la demande; il se prête aux formes les plus souples, les plus inattendues. De plus, il faut noter sa légèreté lors du travail sur le chantier.

Les placages stratifiés ne peuvent être oubliés si l'on évoque les matières plastiques, mais ils ne sont utilisables que collés sur un panneau de bois ou d'aggloméré. Imperméables à l'eau, ils sont proposés dans de nombreux coloris et « dessins ».

### Les produits amiante-ciment

Ils entrent dans la fabrication de plusieurs bardages verticaux et d'éléments modulaires juxtaposables, et offrent, grâce à leurs reliefs très architecturaux, la possibilité de créer des bossages réguliers. Ces bardages et ces éléments peuvent être conservés naturels ou peints.

### Le béton

Lorsque le magasin est conçu en même temps que l'immeuble, le béton pourra rester brut. Le coffrage initial peut comporter une série de plans, de décrochements, une composition spéciale. La beauté du béton n'est plus à démontrer. Il suffira pour l'exalter d'un second matériau bien choisi, d'un éclairage judicieux.

Emailliertes Schaufensterglas in vielen Farbtönen sowie silbriges Glas ergänzen schließlich diese breite Palette der Möglichkeiten.

### Metallbaustoffe

Es gibt viele Arten von unterschiedlichem Aussehen:

Gewöhnliches *Eisen* wird häufig für die Unterkonstruktionen verwendet, auf die eine Verkleidung aufgeschraubt, bzw. mit Klammern oder Haken befestigt wird.

*Verchromtes Metall* mit seiner glänzenden Oberfläche kann für Rahmen und Rohre, für flache oder geschwungene Verkleidungen verwendet werden.

*Kupfer* bietet dieselben Möglichkeiten, muß jedoch mit einem besonderen Schutz gegen Oxydierung versehen werden. Die Kupferverarbeitung gehört in den Bereich des Kunsthandwerks.

*Naturbelassenes Stahlblech* wird im Fassadenbau ebenso häufig gebraucht wie in der modernen Architektur überhaupt. Das Blech kann eine glatte oder eine durch Hämmern strukturierte Oberfläche aufweisen. Die Lackierung erfolgt von Hand oder häufiger als Einbrennlackierung im Ofen und bietet neben allen erdenklichen Farbtönen auch metallisch glänzende Nuancen wie in der Automobilindustrie.

*Nichtrostendes Stahlblech* vereint dieselben Eigenschaften, erfordert jedoch keine weitere Behandlung. Das Material kann für Rahmen und ganze Flächen verwendet werden.

*Aluminium* hat sich im Gebrauch durchgesetzt. Es ist leicht, sauber, einfach und schnell zu bearbeiten. Es wird naturbelassen oder eloxiert (verschiedene Farben) verwendet. Außer für die Herstellung von Rahmen und Rohren eignet sich Aluminium auch für eine breite Skala von Plattenverkleidungen mit vielfältigen und kombinierbaren Profilstärken. Die Herstellungskosten des Materials sind relativ niedrig.

### Holz

Holz ist ein « eigenständiger » Baustoff. Sowohl die Unterkonstruktion wie die Verkleidung einer Fassade kann allein aus Holz bestehen, auf Grund der Vielzahl von Holzarten sowie der zwei verschiedenen, hauptsächlichen Verwendungsmöglichkeiten: entweder massiv, in allen Schnittformen und Stärken lieferbar (Balken, Bretter, Leisten), oder als Furnier (Vertäfelungen nach Maß oder in Standardnormen). Holz ist leicht zu bearbeiten. Falls es nicht gestrichen oder eingefärbt wird (zahlreiche Farbtöne), muß Holz sofort nach seiner Anbringung einen Witterungsschutz in

terracotta, are produced on a quasi-craft basis, which means one can get exactly what one wants in terms of partition units, slabs, and made-to-measure tiles featuring motifs in relief and done in particular colours and finishes.

Conventional brick can be used for the blind portions of a shop front with no further artifice than careful jointing and pointing. Brick paints and lacquers extremely well.

### Plastics

Although certain plastics have been around for some time their qualities are rarely exploited to the full.

Square, rectangular, or relief units are available that can be fitted together to cover continuous surfaces. But modern techniques of folding and thermo-moulding offer a wide variety of possibilities that only the designer who is prepared to leave the beaten track can use to their full advantage. Plastics can be coloured to order and lend themselves to the most fluid and unexpected shapes. Moreover they are very light, which facilitates work on the site.

We cannot mention plastics without mentioning laminated coatings, though these can only be used glued onto plywood or composition panels. They are waterproof and come in a large number of different colours and designs.

### Asbestos-cement products

Abestos cement is used in the manufacture of several types of panelling and assembly unit with highly architectural embossed motifs that make it possible to create a regular relief pattern. They can be left with their natural finish or painted.

### Concrete

When the shop is being built simultaneously with the building any concrete used can be left unrendered. The shuttering can incorporate different planes and levels and even a particular composition. The beauty of unrendered concrete no longer requires demonstration. All it needs is to be set off by a second, well-chosen material and by judicious lighting.

### Plaster and staff

These materials offer numerous possibilities, lending themselves to all kinds of shapes and being easy (for the craftsman, that is) to work. Other materials, lamps, etc., can be bedded in them, and they take paint, lacquer, and smooth or relief coatings very well.

Each of the materials listed here has its own particular application. The majority of them require

*Le plâtre, le staff*
Ces matériaux offrent de multiples possibilités, car ils se prêtent à toutes sortes de formes et se mettent en œuvre avec facilité (de façon artisanale). On peut y encastrer d'autres matériaux, des luminaires, etc. La peinture, la laque, les enduits lisses ou à relief s'y appliquent aisément.

Chacun des matériaux que nous venons d'inventorier a une mise en œuvre qui lui est propre, mais la plupart d'entre eux doivent néanmoins être protégés contre les détériorations internes ou superficielles que pourrait provoquer le ruissellement des eaux de pluie. Dans la construction d'une façade de magasin, l'étude poussée de ce phénomène est importante. A ce titre, l'auvent ou la marquise peuvent quelquefois résoudre la question en canalisant l'eau avec précision.

L'évolution du commerce est réelle, sa physionomie future imprévisible, mais il est souhaitable que durant de longues années encore, le magasin avec ses formes, ses matériaux, ses couleurs, sa lumière, éveille en nous le désir et la joie de flâner au long des rues.
Un peu partout en Europe, les hommes prennent conscience que la rue n'est pas uniquement un couloir à voitures: c'est prometteur et encourageant.

Form eines matten oder glänzenden Firnißanstrichs erhalten.

*Stein*
Dieses Material wird häufig als Fassadenbekleidung verwendet und ist seiner Natur nach in der Stärke sehr variabel. Die Verkleidung wird entweder mit Klammern auf einer Holzunterkonstruktion befestigt oder mit feinem Mörtel direkt auf den Baukörper aufgebracht. Zu den traditionellen Steinen wie Marmor, Schiefer und Granit kommen industriell hergestellte Verbundsteinplatten oder gesägte Kiesel.

*Keramische Produkte*
Dazu gehören Ziegel, Klinker und Backstein, unglasierter und glasierter Ton, Steinzeug und Emailprodukte. Mit Ausnahme einiger Ziegeltypen (Vollziegel oder Hohlziegel) treten diese Materialien sämtlich als Fassadenbekleidung auf.
Einige dieser Baustoffe wie Steinzeug und manche Emailprodukte werden in großem Umfang von der Industrie hergestellt und es empfiehlt sich, unter der breiten Auswahl des vorhandenen Angebots zu wählen. Andere Materialien wie Tonprodukte sind hingegen halb handwerkliche Erzeugnisse und können daher für ganz bestimmte Fälle als Abschlußwandelemente, Module, Platten und Fliesen in den erforderlichen Formaten hergestellt werden; darüber hinaus können sie mit Motiven in Relief verziert sein und in besonderen Farben und Glasuren geliefert werden.
Mit dem traditionellen, in der Architektur verwendeten Backstein können die kompakten Partien einer Fassade aufgeführt werden, ohne daß mehr Aufwand als eine sorgfältige Verfugung nötig wäre. Es wird darauf hingewiesen, daß sich Backstein sehr gut streichen oder lackieren läßt.

*Kunststoffe*
Obwohl sie keine Neuheit auf dem Markt sind, werden Kunststoffprodukte selten in ihren Qualitäten voll ausgeschöpft.
Für die Bekleidung kompakter Wandflächen existieren quadratische, rechteckige oder vertikalverlaufende Module, die nebeneinander gesetzt werden können. Die technischen Verfahren der Faltung und thermischen Formung bieten jedoch eine Vielfalt von Möglichkeiten, die nur durch intensive Forschung außerhalb der bisher beschrittenen Bahnen aufgezeigt werden können. Dieses Material kann nach Bedarf durchgefärbt und in die biegsamsten, überraschendsten Formen gebracht werden. Es bietet ferner den Vorteil seiner Leichtigkeit bei der Arbeit an der Baustelle.

protection against internal or surface damage by running rainwater. This is something that needs to be looked into very carefully when one is building a shop front. A blind or canopy can sometimes solve the problem by channelling the water off.

The evolution of the retail trade is a fact, but what it will look like in future no one can say. Let us hope that for many years to come the shop with its shapes, materials, colour, and lighting will continue to make us want to stroll through the streets of our towns and cities, and to enjoy doing so.
All over Europe people are beginning to wake up to the fact that the street is something more than a place for cars to drive along; it offers both a promise and a stimulus.

Die Kunststoffbeschichtungen dürfen bei der Aufzählung der Plastikmaterialien nicht fehlen, doch sind sie nur in Verbindung mit einer Sperrholz- oder Werksteinunterlage verwendbar. Sie sind wasserundurchlässig und werden in zahlreichen Farben und « Mustern » angeboten.

*Asbestzementprodukte*
Sie finden bei der Herstellung verschiedener vertikaler Plattenverkleidungen und zusammensetzbarer Fassadenmodule Verwendung; auf Grund ihrer architektonisch strukturierten Profile bieten sie die Möglichkeit regelmäßiger Vorsprünge. Diese Plattenelemente und Module können roh belassen oder mit einem Anstrich versehen werden.

*Beton*
Wenn das Geschäft gleichzeitig mit dem Gebäude entsteht, kann der Beton unverputzt bleiben. Schon bei der Verschalung können beliebig ebene Flächen, Vorsprünge, eine spezielle Komposition angelegt werden. Die Schönheit des Betons muß nicht mehr unter Beweis gestellt werden. Um sie zur Geltung zu bringen, genügt die Zusammenstellung mit einem zweiten, gut ausgewählten Material oder auch nur eine durchdachte Beleuchtung.

*Gips, Stuck*
Diese Materialien bieten vielfältige Möglichkeiten, da sie sich (vom Handwerker) relativ einfach und zu beliebigen Formen verarbeiten lassen. Andere Baustoffe, Beleuchtungskörper lassen sich leicht einbauen. Wandfarbe, Lack, glatter und strukturierter Verputz haften gut auf dieser Unterlage.

Von den aufgeführten Materialien hat jedes seine spezifische Verarbeitungsweise, doch benötigen die meisten dennoch einen Schutz gegen innere oder äußere Schäden, die durch Regenwasser hervorgerufen werden. Beim Bau von Geschäftsfassaden ist ein gründliches Studium dieses Phänomens wichtig. In diesem Zusammenhang können manchmal ein Vordach oder eine Markise zur Lösung des Problems beitragen, indem sie das Wasser abfangen und präzise ableiten.

Die Entwicklung des Handels ist eine Tatsache, seine Erscheinungsform in der Zukunft unvorhersehbar. Es bleibt jedoch zu wünschen, daß das Geschäft mit seinem Formenreichtum, mit seinen Materialien, Farben und Lichteffekten in uns noch lange Zeit den Wunsch nach einem Bummel durch die Straßen weckt und Freude daran wachhält.
Vielerorts in Europa wird man sich bewußt, daß die Straße nicht nur für Autos da ist: das ist ermutigend und vielversprechend.

France
Frankreich
France

# 1. Castillo, Paris

Eric Lieuré, Designer, Paris

Ce magasin de couture est installé dans une ancienne et célèbre galerie de peinture. La façade primitive du XIXᵉ siècle, décorée de bas-reliefs et percée de trois arcades, n'a pas été modifiée. L'actuelle devanture est en retrait de quelques mètres, créant ainsi une agréable galerie couverte. Par souci de classicisme, les trois nouvelles ouvertures sont axées sur les trois arcades. L'accès est au centre. Ces ouvertures aux angles arrondis occupent toute la hauteur du volume, donnant jour à la fois sur les vitrines, le sas d'entrée et une mezzanine intérieure. La structure des ouvertures est réalisée en laiton poli; le fond sur lequel elles se détachent est en métal laqué satiné. Trois groupes de spots directionnels éclairent la galerie.

Dieses Modegeschäft ist in einer alten und berühmten Bildergalerie untergebracht. Die ursprüngliche, mit Flachreliefs verzierte und von drei Arkaden durchbrochene Fassade aus dem 19. Jahrhundert blieb unverändert. Die jetzige Auslage ist einige Meter nach rückwärts versetzt, wodurch eine ansprechende überdachte Galerie entsteht. Um das klassizistische Gesicht zu erhalten, wurden die drei neuen Maueröffnungen genau auf die drei Arkaden ausgerichtet. Der Eingang liegt in der Mitte. Die in den Ecken abgerundeten Öffnungen nehmen die ganze Höhe des Raumes ein, so daß gleichzeitig die Auslagen, die Eingangszone und ein innen eingebautes Zwischengeschoß Licht erhalten. Die Strukturelemente der Öffnungen sind in poliertem Messing ausgeführt, der umgebende Hintergrund besteht aus mattlackiertem Metall. Drei Gruppen fest ausgerichteter Spots beleuchten die Galerie.

This fashion shop occupies the former premises of a well-known art gallery. The original nineteenth-century façade with its bas-relief decoration and its three arches has been left unaltered. The present shop front is set back several metres, creating a delightful covered gallery. To preserve the classical effect the three new apertures are aligned with the three arches, the entrance being in the middle. They have rounded corners and occupy the whole height of the premises, lighting the display windows, the vestibule, and a mezzanine inside the shop. The structure of the apertures is executed in polished brass and the wall they stand out from in metal painted with a satin finish. The gallery is lit by three groups of movable spots.

| Longueur de la façade | 13 m |
|---|---|
| Hauteur | 5,15 m |
| Profondeur de la galerie | 3,50 m |

| Fassadenlänge | 13 m |
|---|---|
| Höhe | 5,15 m |
| Tiefe der Galerie | 3,50 m |

| Frontage | 13 m |
|---|---|
| Height | 5.15 m |
| Depth of gallery | 3.50 m |

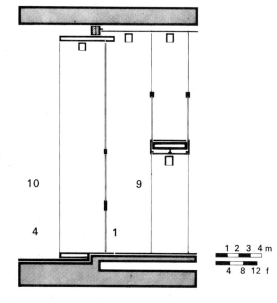

B

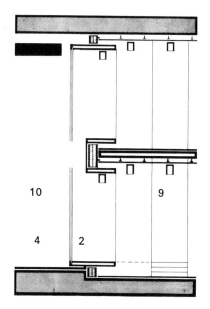

A

1. La façade avec les trois arcades conservées

1. Die Fassade mit den drei erhaltenen Arkaden

1. The façade with the three original arches

3

2. L'ouverture centrale avec la porte d'entrée; en partie supérieure, la mezzanine intérieure
3. La galerie et la porte d'entrée
4. Une ouverture latérale avec sa vitrine inférieure et vue sur la mezzanine intérieure

2. Die zentrale Maueröffnung mit der Eingangstüre, im oberen Teil das eingebaute Zwischengeschoß
3. Galerie und Eingangstüre
4. Seitliche Maueröffnung mit der unteren Auslage und Blick auf das Zwischengeschoß

2. The middle aperture, showing the entrance below and the mezzanine above
3. The gallery and the entrance door
4. One of the side apertures, showing the display window and the mezzanine above

2

## 2. Roche Bobois, Paris    Annie Tribel, Designer, Paris

Situé dans une construction d'angle, ce magasin de mobilier et d'articles de décoration devait être visible de la grande avenue toute proche. L'immeuble ne présentait pas un caractère très affirmé. Toutefois, certains angles et profils de l'architecture ont discrètement inspiré la composition générale qui se singularise par sa série de «marquises», supports des enseignes lumineuses. Ces marquises sont au nombre de cinq; l'une d'elles surplombe l'entrée placée dans l'angle. Elles sont réalisées, comme les panneaux dans lesquels elles s'encastrent, en polyester et en fibre de verre. La jonction des éléments est volontairement très marquée, ainsi que leur fixation sur l'armature générale métallique. Outre la glace des vitrines, le polyester et le plexiglas, l'acier inoxydable est le quatrième matériau utilisé pour les huisseries et les poignées des deux portes d'entrée.

Dieses in einem Eckgebäude gelegene Geschäft für Möbel und Inneneinrichtungen mußte von der nahe vorbeiführenden Hauptstraße her gut sichtbar sein. Das Gebäude zeigte keinen besonders ausgeprägten Charakter. Dennoch lieferten bestimmte Winkelpartien und Profile der Architektur Anhaltspunkte für die Gesamtkomposition, die durch eine Reihe von «Markisen», an denen Leuchtschriften angebracht sind, eine auffallende Note erhält. Von den insgesamt fünf Markisen überdacht eine den an der Ecke liegenden Eingang. Die Markisen bestehen wie die Platten, in die sie eingesetzt sind, aus Polyester und Glasfiber. Die Verbindungsstellen der einzelnen Elemente sind betont sichtbar, ebenso wie deren Befestigung auf der Gesamtumkleidung aus Metall. Als viertes Material neben dem Schaufensterglas der Auslagen, neben Polyester und Plexiglas, steht nichtrostender Stahl, der für die Rahmen und Griffe der beiden Eingangstüren verwendet wurde.

Occupying a corner site, this furniture and decoration accessories shop had to be visible from the nearby avenue. The building has no particular character, but certain angles and lines of the architecture have subtly inspired the general composition with its distinctive series of canopies containing illuminated signs. There are five of these in all, including one over the corner entrance. These and the panels framing them are executed in polyester and fibreglass. The joints between the elements are deliberately emphasized, as is the method of attachment to the metal framework behind. As well as glass for the windows, polyester, and fibreglass, a fourth material, namely stainless steel, is used for the door frames and door bars.

| Longueur de la façade | 28,50 m |
|---|---|
| Hauteurs | 5,30/4 m |

| Fassadenlänge | 28,50 m |
|---|---|
| Höhenmaße | 5,30/4 m |

| Frontage | 28.50 m |
|---|---|
| Heights | 5.30/4 m |

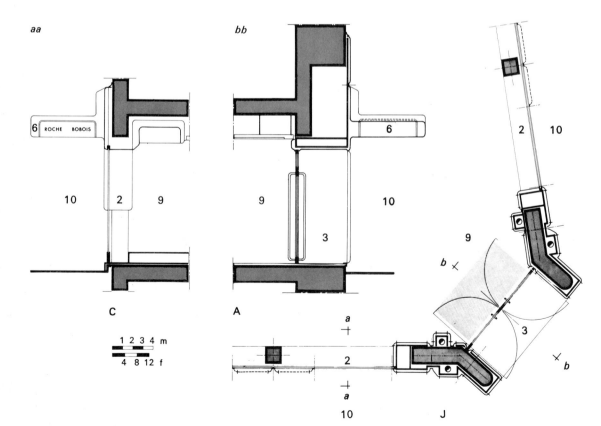

1. Succession des marquises

1. Die Reihe der aufeinanderfolgenden Markisen

1. The row of canopies

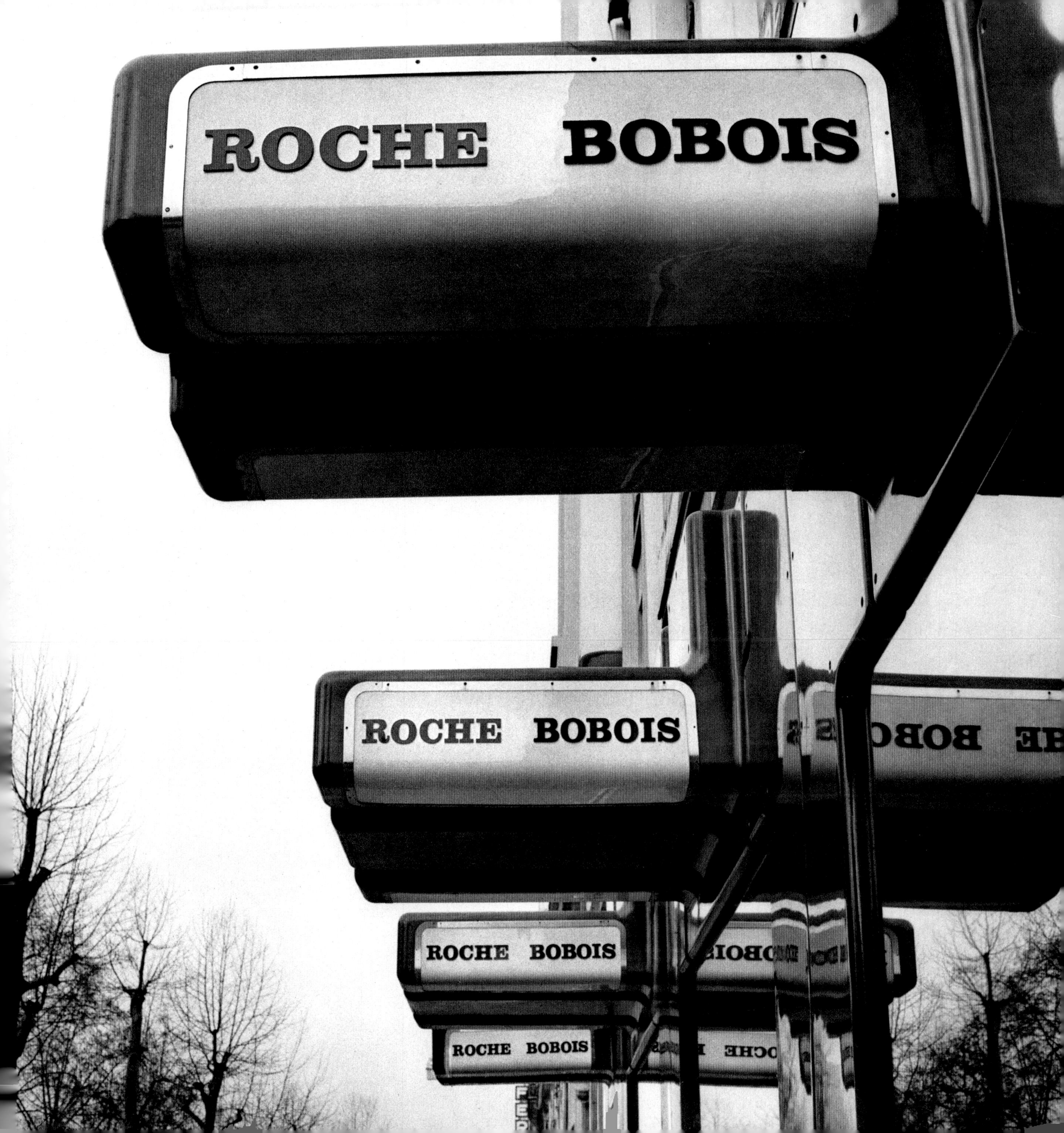
ROCHE BOBOIS
ROCHE BOBOIS
ROCHE BOBOIS
ROCHE BOBOIS

2

3

4

2. La façade générale; l'entrée est située dans l'angle
3. Les formes de la composition et l'architecture existante
4. Le jeu des panneaux sur l'angle de la façade
5. L'emboîtement de plusieurs panneaux et des marquises

2. Die Hauptfassade mit dem an der Ecke liegenden Eingang
3. Das Zusammenspiel der Fassadenelemente und der Architektur
4. Spiel der zusammengesetzten Platten an der Ecke der Fassade
5. Die kompositorische Zusammensetzung mehrerer Platten und der Markisen

2. The main front, showing the entrance on the corner
3. The shapes used for the shop front match the existing architecture
4. Detail of the corner, showing how the panels fit together
5. The jointing of the panels and canopies

## 3.  John Bell, Paris

### Serfaty, Designer, Paris

L'architecture générale de l'immeuble où est installé ce magasin de vêtements comportait un pilier de soutènement assez large. Celui-ci n'a pas été dissimulé sous un habillage; il reste au contraire très évident. La porte d'entrée centrale est nettement en retrait du mur de la maison. Les vitrines affleurent cette façade aux deux angles extérieurs de la construction, et par une série de décrochements, elles rejoignent le niveau de la porte. Ces vitrines sont insérées dans des caissons en polyester armé de fibre de verre. Le caisson aux lignes courbes qui surplombe la double porte d'entrée et qui se prolonge à l'intérieur a été traité dans le même matériau. Au-dessus des caissons des vitrines et de la porte, les imposses fixées en retrait sont en glace claire. Sous les vitrines, le soubassement est en maçonnerie traditionnelle. Le mur sur rue et le pilier ont reçu une finition en ciment-pierre.
L'éclairage de la petite galerie est assuré par des appareils diffusants. A l'extérieur, quelques spots directionnels sont fixés latéralement sur des cadres en avancée. Les graphismes de signalisation sont en tôle laquée et en métal chromé.

Die architektonische Anlage des Hauses, in dem dieses Fachgeschäft für Herrenbekleidung liegt, weist einen ziemlich breiten Stützpfeiler auf. Er wurde jedoch nicht mit einer Verkleidung unsichtbar gemacht, sondern blieb im Gegenteil in der Front sichtbar. Die in der Mitte liegende Eingangstüre ist deutlich hinter die Außenmauer des Hauses zurückversetzt. Diese Verschiebung der Fassade wird durch die Vitrinen wieder ausgeglichen, die, an den beiden äußeren Enden des Hauses beginnend, durch eine Reihe von Vorsprüngen an die Ebene der Eingangstüre anschließen. Diese Vitrinen sind in Kästen aus glasfaserarmierten Polyester eingesetzt. Das abgerundete Gehäuse, das die zweiflügelige Eingangstüre überdacht und sich spiegelbildlich nach innen fortsetzt, besteht aus demselben Material. Oberhalb der über den Schaufenstern und Türen eingefügten Kästen befinden sich etwas zurückgesetzte Oberlichter aus Glas. Die als Stützstruktur dienende Partie unterhalb der Schaufenster ist in konventionellem Mauerwerk ausgeführt. Die Fassadenmauer und der Pfeiler erhielten einen Feinverputz aus Steinzement.
Die kleine Galerie erhält ihr Licht durch breitstreuende Beleuchtungskörper. In der Außenzone sind an vorspringenden Partien seitlich einige fest fixierte Spots angebracht. Die Ladenbeschilderung besteht aus lackiertem Blech und verchromtem Metall.

The structure of the building housing this clothing shop includes a fairly broad supporting pier that, rather than being concealed in any way, has been left very much in evidence. The entrance is set some way back from the line of the façade. The display windows, starting from that line at the sides, run back in a series of steps to meet the centrally situated door. The display windows are set in polyester boxes with fibreglass reinforcement. The rounded box flanking and overhanging the double entrance door and extending inside the shop is executed in the same materials. The fixed, recessed transom windows above the boxes framing display windows and door are of clear glass. The contrasting wall below and supporting the display windows is of traditional masonry. The street wall and the pillar have a stone-cement rendering.
The little gallery is lit by floods. Outside a number of movable spots are mounting on projecting brackets at the sides. The signs are done in enamelled sheet steel and chromium-plated metal.

| Longueur de la façade | 9,35 m | Fassadenlänge | 9,35 m | Frontage | 9.35 m |
| Hauteur | 4,30 m | Höhe | 4,30 m | Height | 4.30 m |

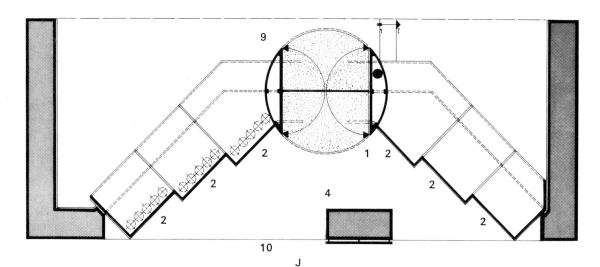

1. La porte d'entrée et son caisson. Notons l'éclairage latéral

1. Die Eingangstüre mit dem darüberliegenden Gehäuse. Man beachte die seitlich angebrachte Beleuchtung

1. The entrance door and the box that frames it. Note the lighting from the side

1

2. La façade
3. La partie supérieure des vitrines et le plafond de la galerie

2. Die Fassade
3. Der obere Teil der Vitrinen und die Decke der Galerie

2. View of the whole shop front
3. The upper part of the display windows and a portion of the gallery ceiling

2

## 4.  Alexandre Savin, Paris        A. Savin, Designer, Paris

Ce magasin de couture est situé à l'angle de deux rues. La finition de la façade a été traitée en ciment-pierre finement lissé. Aucun habillage ne vient modifier le rythme des ouvertures — portes et vitrines. Par contre, la conception de ces dernières est très élaborée: chaque jeu de vitrines est composé sur deux plans. Les glaces claires des parties saillantes sont galbées sur les angles. Les huisseries sont en laiton poli avec une finition le protégeant du ternissement. Elles ont un profil assez épais et généreux. Les angles intérieurs sont arrondis. La partie supérieure des vitrines en avancée est coiffée d'un mini-auvent inspiré du store-corbeille. Il est composé de lames en acier chromé brillant, placées en recouvrement. Le seuil des portes est en marbre; la hauteur de la marche se prolonge autour de la façade sous forme de plinthe en retrait. Le nom du couturier constitue l'enseigne.

Dieser Modesalon liegt am Schnittpunkt zweier Straßen. Die Fassade wurde mit sorgfältig geglättetem Steinzement verputzt. Keinerlei Verkleidung unterbricht den Rhythmus der Maueröffnungen — Türen und Schaufenster — deren Komposition allerdings sehr durchdacht angelegt ist: Jede Schaufenstergruppe weist zwei Ebenen von verschiedener Tiefe auf. Die Glasscheiben der hervorstehenden Partien sind in den Ecken rund ausgeformt. Die Rahmen bestehen aus poliertem Messing mit einem Schutzüberzug gegen Verwitterung. Ihr Profil ist ziemlich stark und großzügig. Die Ecken sind auf der Innenseite abgerundet. Über dem oberen Teil der vorspringenden Schaufensterpartien befindet sich jeweils ein baldachinartiges Vordach. Es besteht aus einander überlagernden Lamellen aus glanzverchromtem Stahl. Die Türschwellen sind in Marmor ausgeführt, der sich in Stufenhöhe als Verkleidung an der Fassade entlangzieht. Der Name des Modeschöpfers stellt die Ladenbeschilderung dar.

The façade of this corner-site fashion shop has a smooth rendering of stone cement. No dressing modifies the rhythm of the apertures—doors and windows—but in conception they are extremely sophisticated. Each group of display windows is designed in two planes. The clear panes of the projecting portions are rounded at the sides. The frames are executed in polished brass with an anti-tarnish finish. They are quite generous in section, with the inside corners rounded. The projecting portions of the windows are capped by miniature canopies whose design is based on the basket blind. They are constructed of overlapping strips of shiny chromium-plated steel. The doorsteps are of marble, and the line of the step is continued round the façade in the form of a recessed plinth. The couturier's name figures as the sign.

| Longueur de la façade | 17 m | Fassadenlänge | 17 m | Frontage | 17 m |
|---|---|---|---|---|---|
| Hauteur | 2,65 m | Höhe | 2,65 m | Height | 2.65 m |

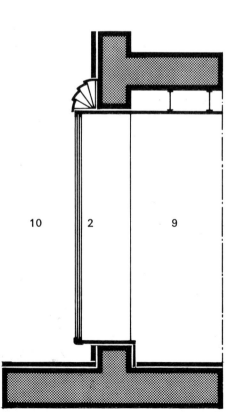

B

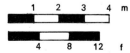

1

2

3

4

5

Pour ce magasin de prêt-à-porter, le designer a conçu une façade-sculpture. Elle est constituée par la superposition de fractions de cylindres dont les diamètres sont décroissants. Ces volumes encadrent un panneau vertical toute hauteur à la base duquel s'ouvre une porte à double battant en glace claire, précédée d'un petit sas extérieur. Les vitrines, de la même hauteur que les portes, sont galbées; elles ne sont séparées du trottoir que par une fine huisserie métallique. Toutes les parties non vitrées, courbes et planes, sont faites de plaques de métal chromé sur armature en menuiserie. Les pilastres extérieurs, leurs retours latéraux et le bandeau sont traités en ciment-pierre.
Sur le bandeau, la raison sociale est réalisée en métal chromé avec éclairage intérieur. Le même graphisme se retrouve peint sur les glaces de la porte d'entrée. Deux séries de spots, fixés sur des armatures métalliques en avancée, sont placées de part et d'autre de la composition. Ces spots assurent l'éclairage d'ambiance et multiplient les points de brillance sur les surfaces chromées et la glace.

Für dieses Konfektionshaus wurde vom Designer eine starkmodellierte Fassade entworfen. Sie besteht aus einander überlagernden Zylinderfragmenten, deren Durchmesser abnehmen. Diese Volumen umrahmen eine in ganzer Höhe durchgehende, senkrechte Platte, an deren unterem Ende sich eine zweiflügelige Eingangstüre aus Glas befindet, der ein kleiner Außenraum vorgelagert ist. Die Vitrinen zeigen dieselbe Höhe wie die Türen und sind gebaucht. Von dem vorbeiführenden Gehsteig sind sie nur durch einen dünnen Metallrahmen getrennt. Alle nichtverglasten Flächen, gleich ob gekrümmt oder eben, bestehen aus verchromten Metallplatten, die auf eine Holzverkleidung aufgesetzt sind. Die äußeren Stützpfeiler, ihre Seitenflächen und die Fassadenblende sind in Steinzement ausgeführt.
Auf der Fassadenblende ist der Firmenname in verchromten Metallbuchstaben mit einer Innenbeleuchtung angebracht. Dieselbe Beschriftung wurde auf die Glasscheiben der Eingangstüre aufgemalt. Zu beiden Seiten der Auslagenfront befinden sich in zwei Reihen angeordnete Spotlights, die auf vorstehenden Metallflächen befestigt sind. Diese Spots liefern die allgemeine Beleuchtung und erzeugen eine Vielfalt von Glanzlichtern in den verchromten Teilen und im Schaufensterglas.

This ready-to-wear shop has been given a sculptural front made up of fractions of cylinders of progressively decreasing diameter piled one on top of another. These volumes flank a vertical panel running the whole height of the front, the lower part consisting of a double door of clear glass preceded by a small open vestibule. The display windows, which are the same height as the door, are curved. Only a thin metal frame separates them from the pavement. All non-glazed portions, flat and curved, are executed in sheets of chromium-plated metal mounted on a wooden framework. The outside pilasters, their returns, and the facia above are rendered with stone cement. The name of the shop figures on the facia in chromium-plated metal lettering lit from inside. The same sign is repeated in paint on the glass doors. Two rows of spots mounted on projecting metal brackets flank the whole composition, providing ambient lighting and picking out innumerable highlights in the glass and chromium-plating.

| Longueur de la façade | 10 m |
| Hauteur | 6,40 m |

| Fassadenlänge | 10 m |
| Höhe | 6,40 m |

| Frontage | 10 m |
| Height | 6.40 m |

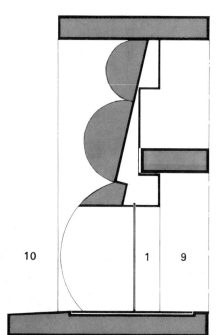

10      1   9

1 2 3 4 m

4 8 12 f

A

1. La façade et l'immeuble
2. L'angle des vitrines et de la porte d'entrée

1. Die Geschäftsfassade und das Haus
2. Der Winkel zwischen den Schaufenstern und der Eingangstüre

1. View of the shop front showing part of the building
2. The angle between display window and door

1

2

3

4

3. L'angle des vitrines et du retour des pilastres latéraux
4. Les courbes des volumes et le panneau vertical du centre

3. Der Winkel zwischen den Schaufenstern und den Seitenflächen der Stützpfeiler
4. Die geschwungenen Linien der zylindrischen Körper und die senkrechte Platte der Fassadenfront

3. The angle between display window and pilaster return
4. The rounded volumes and the vertical central panel

5. Les deux vitrines et le sas extérieur central

5. Die beiden Schaufenster und der in der Mitte liegende Außenraum

5. The two display windows and the open vestibule between them

## 6.   Galerie Roudillon, Paris  Georges Roudillon, Designer, Paris

Cette devanture très sobre et bien structurée est celle d'une galerie d'objets archéologiques. L'ouverture d'origine percée dans le gros œuvre était haute et étroite. Lors de l'aménagement de la façade, le caractère de verticalité a été maintenu, mais la composition a été élargie grâce à des habillages latéraux en glace émaillée qui lui confèrent une rigueur en harmonie avec la qualité des objets présentés. La frise supérieure existait avant les travaux. La partie centrale, entièrement en glace claire, se compose de la vitrine proprement dite et de la porte qui se trouve en retrait, créant ainsi un petit sas ouvert où se trouve, latéralement et en réserve dans l'épaisseur du mur, l'unique signalisation de la galerie. En plus de la glace claire et émaillée, les matériaux sont l'aluminium, le marbre blanc et le staff laqué.

Diese sehr nüchterne und klar gegliederte Auslage gehört zu einer Galerie für antike Kunst. Die ursprüngliche Eingangstüre des Bauwerks war hoch und schmal. Beim Umbau der Fassade blieb der vertikale Gesamteindruck erhalten, doch wurde die Anlage durch seitlich angebrachte Verkleidungen aus farbigem Glas verbreitert, deren strenge Wirkung dem Charakter der ausgestellten Objekte entspricht. Das Gebälk über der Eingangstüre war bereits vor dem Umbau vorhanden. Der mittlere Teil besteht ganz aus durchsichtigem Schaufensterglas und enthält die eigentliche Auslage und die Eingangstüre; diese ist etwas nach rückwärts versetzt, wodurch ein kleiner offener Raum entsteht, in dem seitlich und etwas in die Mauer eingelassen, das einzige Namensschild der Galerie angebracht ist. Neben klarem und farbigem Glas wurden die Materialien Aluminium, weißer Marmor und lackierter Stuckgips verwendet.

This restrained and finely structured composition fronts a gallery of archaeological objects. The original aperture was tall and narrow and this verticality has been retained in the design of the shop front, but the composition has been broadened by means of lateral panels of enamelled glass that give it a severity in keeping with the objects displayed. The frieze above was there before the conversion. The central portion, entirely of clear glass, comprises the display window proper and the door. This is recessed, leaving a small open vestibule on one side of which, let into the wall, is the gallery's only sign. In addition to clear and enamelled glass, the other materials used are aluminium, white marble, and painted plaster.

| Longueur de la façade | 3,90 m |
|---|---|
| Hauteur | 4,60 m |
| Profondeur du sas | 0,70 m |

| Fassadenlänge | 3,90 m |
|---|---|
| Höhe | 4,60 m |
| Tiefe des Vorraums | 0,70 m |

| Frontage | 3.90 m |
|---|---|
| Height | 4.60 m |
| Depth of vestibule | 0.70 m |

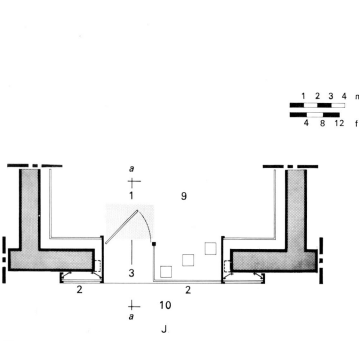

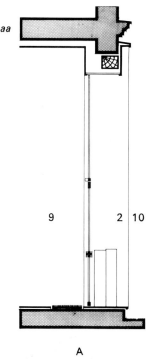

1.  Vue de l'intérieur sur le petit sas extérieur
2.  La poignée en aluminium de la porte
3.  La façade générale

1.  Blick von innen auf den kleinen äußeren Vorraum
2.  Der Aluminiumgriff der Eingangstüre
3.  Gesamtansicht der Fassade

1.  The small open vestibule seen from inside
2.  The aluminium door-handle
3.  View of the whole shop front

1

2

3

## 7.  Jardinage Sélection, Paris       Annie Tribel, Designer, Paris

Le commerce de graines, de produits et d'outils de jardinage ne peut se concevoir sans une présentation extérieure. Cette particularité a orienté esthétiquement l'aspect du magasin. Une marquise assez large surplombe la totalité de la façade. Elle fait partie d'une structure réalisée en bois laqué. Les plaques métalliques assurant la liaison des différents éléments et les tirants dont la tension est réglable sont volontairement apparents. Cette marquise est constituée d'une face en plastique ondulé canalisant les eaux de pluie et d'une sous-face composée de panneaux laqués. Au centre, deux panneaux sont translucides pour laisser filtrer la lumière du jour et celle de rampes fluorescentes lorsque la nuit est venue. Un éclairage supplémentaire est assuré par quelques spots directionnels.
Plusieurs portes coulissantes et pivotantes composent la façade proprement dite. Les cadres de ces huisseries sont plaqués de lamifié.
Aucune raison sociale n'est apparente. Le magasin se signale au passant par ses couleurs et son étalage.

Der Handel mit Samen, Gartenbedarf und Gartengeräten kommt ohne eine Auslage im Freien nicht aus. Dieser Gesichtspunkt war für die Gestaltung des Ladens in ästhetischer Hinsicht bestimmend. Über die ganze Länge der Fassade zieht sich ein ziemlich breites Vordach hin, das Bestandteil eines in lackiertem Holz ausgeführten Gerüsts ist. Die Metallplatten, durch die die einzelnen Elemente zusammengehalten werden, sowie die verstellbaren Zugvorrichtungen sind bewußt sichtbar gelassen. Das Vordach besteht auf der Oberseite aus gewelltem Kunststoff, auf dem das Regenwasser abläuft, auf der Unterseite aus lackierten Platten. Im Mittelteil sind zwei durchsichtige Platten eingesetzt, die das Tageslicht und nachts das Licht der Leuchtstoffröhren eindringen lassen. Mehrere festmontierte Spots sorgen für zusätzliche Beleuchtung. Die eigentliche Fassade setzt sich aus mehreren Schiebe- und Drehtüren zusammen. Die Rahmen der Gestelle sind mit Metallfolie überzogen.
Auf ein Firmenschild wurde verzichtet. Der Laden fällt dem Passanten durch seine Farbigkeit und seine Auslagen auf.

The seed and garden-tool retail trade is inconceivable without some form of outside display, a fact that was not without its influence on the design of this shop front. A fairly broad canopy runs the whole length of the front, forming part of a structure executed in painted wood. The metal plates joining the various elements and the adjustable-tension guy-rods are deliberately emphasized. The canopy consists of an upper face of corrugated plastic to channel the rainwater and a lower face of painted panels. The two middle panels are translucent in order to let the daylight through and, at night, the light of the fluorescent strips. Supplementary lighting is provided by a number of movable spots. The actual shop front consists of a number of sliding and pivoting doors in frames covered with laminated plastic.
There is no name displayed, the shop relying on its colourful displays of goods to attract the attention of passers-by.

| Longueur de la façade | 9,40 m | Fassadenlänge | 9,40 m | Frontage | 9.40 m |
|---|---|---|---|---|---|
| Hauteur | 4 m | Höhe | 4 m | Height | 4 m |

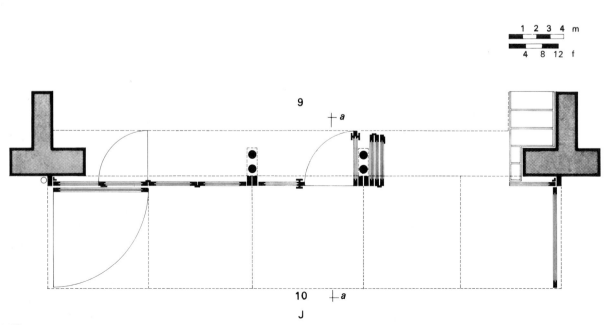

J

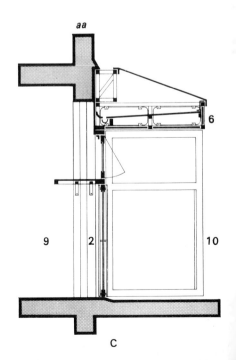

C

1

2

1. L'étalage et les portes de la façade
2. La présentation extérieure sous la marquise

1. Auslage und Türen der Fassade
2. Die Auslage im Freien unter dem Vordach

1. The shop front, showing the display window and the doors
2. The outside display under the canopy

3. L'accrochage de la marquise
4. La marquise et sa partie centrale translucide

3. Die Aufhängevorrichtung des Vordaches
4. Das Vordach mit dem durchsichtigen Mittelteil

3. Detail of the canopy attachment
4. The canopy, showing the translucent middle portion

3

4

1. Une porte d'entrée en angle vue de l'intérieur

1. Im Winkel liegende Eingangstüre, von innen her gesehen

1. One of the obliquely placed doors, seen from inside

2. Les vitrines en angle
3. La façade dans sa totalité

2. Die gewinkelten Schaufenster
3. Die gesamte Ladenfassade

2. The side display windows form angles
3. View of the whole shop front

## 9. Claude Carraz, Paris          Michel Boyer, Designer, Paris

La façade de cette réalisation destinée à un magasin de chaussures est particulièrement symétrique. L'entrée centrale est en retrait du niveau extérieur, créant un sas. Le soubassement formant la marche et le sol de ce sas sont réalisés en plaques d'aggloméré de marbre. Les deux vitrines en glace claire qui occupent toute la hauteur disponible sont inscrites dans un cadre en aluminium. Toutes les autres surfaces de la façade, les retours intérieurs du sas et la porte d'entrée sont en glace teintée. Cette glace est arrondie dans tous les angles verticaux, ce qui confère à l'ensemble une douceur appréciable.

Pour assurer un éclairage d'ambiance, des lignes de tubes néon sont superposées dans des blocs en plexiglas teinté, ces derniers étant placés à l'intérieur au centre de chacune des vitrines et à l'extérieur au centre du sas. La signalisation centrale est composée de lettres en altuglas serties dans le caisson supérieur; elles sont éclairées de l'intérieur. Le sigle de la maison a inspiré le dessin de la poignée de la porte d'entrée.

| | |
|---|---|
| Longueur de la façade | 7,60 m |
| Hauteur | 4 m |

Die Fassade dieses Schuhgeschäfts ist symmetrisch angelegt. Der in der Mitte liegende Eingang ist hinter die Außenfront zurückgesetzt. Die Treppenstufe und der Boden des Vorraums bestehen aus Kunstmarmorplatten. Die beiden Glasvitrinen nehmen die ganze verfügbare Höhe ein und werden von einem Aluminiumrahmen eingefaßt. Alle anderen Flächen der Fassade, die Innenseiten des Vorraums und die Eingangstüre bestehen aus farbigem Glas. Diese Glasflächen sind an sämtlichen vertikalen Kanten abgerundet, wodurch ein ansprechender Gesamteindruck entsteht.

Die Beleuchtung erfolgt durch mehrere, in Reihen übereinandergesetzte Neonröhren in Blöcken aus farbigem Plexiglas, welche im Inneren jeweils in der Mitte der beiden Auslagen und im Außenbereich im Zentrum des Vorraums angebracht sind. Der Firmenname in der Mitte besteht aus Schmelzglasbuchstaben, die in die Füllung über der Türe eingesetzt und mit einer Innenbeleuchtung ausgestattet sind. Das Firmensymbol diente als Vorlage für den Entwurf des Handgriffs der Eingangstüre.

| | |
|---|---|
| Fassadenlänge | 7,60 m |
| Höhe | 4 m |

The most distinctive feature of this shoe shop front is its symmetry. The entrance is in the middle and is recessed, forming a vestibule. The base constituting the step and the floor of the latter is made of slabs of marble agglomerate. The two clear-glass display windows occupying the whole height of the front are mounted in aluminium frames. The remaining façade surfaces as well as the sides of the vestibule and the door are of tinted glass. On the corners of the windows and in the corners between windows and door the glass is rounded, which considerably softens the general aspect of the composition.

Ambient lighting is provided by lines of neon tubes placed one on top of another in tinted-plexiglass blocks, one in the middle of each display window inside and one outside in the middle of the vestibule. The sign is made up of altuglass lettering mounted on a panel above the entrance and lit from inside. The door-handle is inspired by the firm's device.

| | |
|---|---|
| Frontage | 7.60 m |
| Height | 4 m |

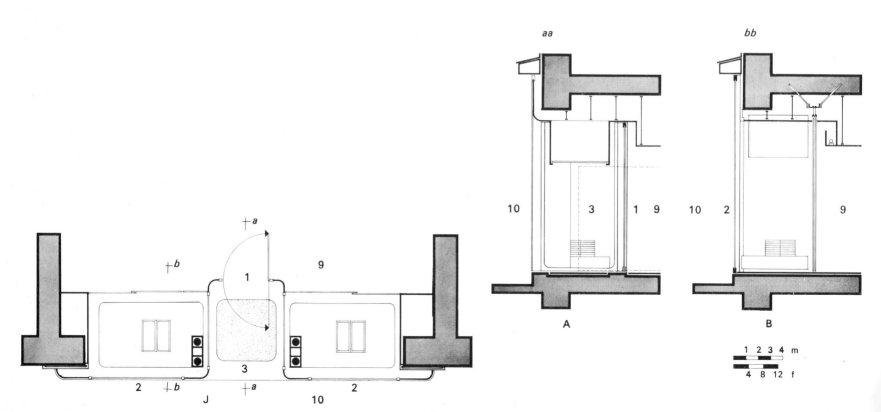

1

1. La façade
2. Une des vitrines; à gauche, l'entrée

1. Die Fassade
2. Eines der Schaufenster, links der Eingang

1. View of the whole shop front
2. One of the display windows, with the entrance on the left

2

3. L'intérieur du sas
4. Détail d'une vitrine et de l'habillage
   en glace teintée
5. Le plafond du sas et la signalisation

3. Das Innere des Vorraums
4. Detailansicht einer Auslage und der
   Verkleidung aus farbigem Glas
5. Die Decke des Vorraums und der
   Firmenname

3. Detail of the vestibule
4. Detail of a display window and the
   tinted-glass facing
5. The ceiling of the vestibule, showing
   the sign

3

4

Voici un magasin d'optique très séduisant, bien qu'il n'offre aux passants que deux étroites vitrines dont le graphisme est repris latéralement.
La construction, incluse dans un immeuble actuel, est asymétrique. Elle se compose de deux blocs réalisés en maçonnerie traditionnelle avec finition crépie. Le bloc comprenant les vitrines est le plus saillant. Le bloc arrière, peint d'un ton plus foncé, est dissocié du mur latéral par une fine meurtrière laissant filtrer la lumière, tout comme la porte en glace, barrée d'une large poignée en bois naturel. La position des deux blocs construits — qui se prolongent à l'intérieur — justifie la mise en place d'un tapis-brosse reprenant en partie les formes arrondies caractéristiques de cette composition.

Dieses Beispiel eines Optikerfachgeschäfts ist sehr reizvoll, obwohl sich dem Passanten nur zwei schmale Auslagen bieten, deren graphische Struktur sich an den Seiten wiederholt.
Die asymmetrische Konstruktion in einem modernen Gebäude besteht aus zwei Blöcken, die in konventionellem Mauerwerk mit Feinverputz ausgeführt sind. Der «Vitrinenblock» springt weiter vor. Der zurückgesetzte Block ist in einem dunkleren Ton gestrichen und wird von der Seitenmauer durch einen schmalen Schlitz getrennt, der, wie die mit einem breiten Naturholzgriff bestückte Glastüre, das Licht eindringen läßt. Die Lage der beiden sich im Inneren fortsetzenden Blöcke zueinander gab Anlaß zur Anbringung einer Türmatte, in der sich die charakteristischen abgerundeten Formen dieser Komposition bruchstückhaft wiederholen.

This is a most attractive optician's shop although all it offers the passer-by is two narrow windows the design of which is echoed on the side wall.
The shop forms part of a modern building and the shop front is asymmetrical in composition. It consists of two blocks of traditional masonry, rough-rendered. The one containing the display windows projects farther than the other, which is also painted a darker colour. The latter block is separated from the side wall by a slit window admitting daylight, as does the glass door with its broad horizontal handle of natural wood. Between the two blocks of masonry, which extend inside the shop, a doormat takes up the rounded shapes that characterize the whole composition.

| | | | | | |
|---|---|---|---|---|---|
| Longueur de la façade | 4,40 m | Fassadenbreite | 4,40 m | Frontage | 4.40 m |
| Hauteur | 2,55 m | Höhe | 2,55 m | Height | 2.55 m |
| Profondeur du hall | 1,60 m | Höhe der Halle | 1,60 m | Depth of vestibule | 1.60 m |

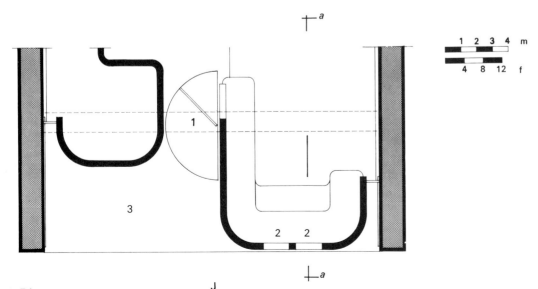

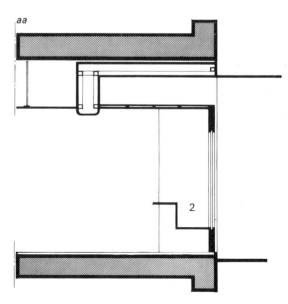

J                                                                                              B

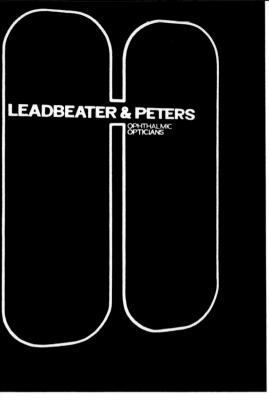

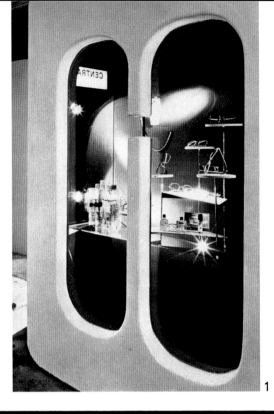

1. Les deux vitrines
2. Une vue générale; à gauche, la fine meurtrière verticale

1. Die beiden Vitrinen
2. Gesamtansicht. Links der schmale, vertikale Mauerschlitz

1. The two display windows
2. View of the whole shop front. Note the tall slit window on the left

voor keukens
alles in hout

Leicht

## 11.  Denis Deux, Amsterdam    Hans C. Niemeyer, Arch., Amsterdam

Cette composition résolument actuelle, destinée à un magasin de mode, exalte parfaitement la beauté rigoureuse de la façade ancienne de la maison du XVIIIe siècle qui l'abrite.
L'entrée est constituée d'un petit hall dont le sol, surélevé de deux marches, est tendu d'un tapis de caoutchouc rainuré. De part et d'autre de ce hall, deux vitrines se font face. L'une d'elles jouxte le seul pilier de la construction générale. Visibles sur deux côtés et construites en tôle d'acier poli, ces vitrines s'inscrivent dans une structure générale en bois avec une finition de peinture laquée. L'auvent aux formes souples est bâti et fini de la même manière. Sa face inférieure prolonge le plafond du hall. Un graphisme peint décore les battants de la porte d'entrée; il se retrouve sous forme de bandes métalliques en applique sur l'auvent et encadre les lettres également en métal. Le tout est étudié en étroite harmonie avec l'architecture de la maison.

Diese entschieden moderne Komposition, die für einen Modeladen geschaffen wurde, bringt die strenge Schönheit der antiken Fassade dieses Hauses aus dem 18. Jahrhundert vollendet zur Geltung. Zu beiden Seiten der zwei Treppenstufen erhöht liegenden kleinen Halle, die mit einem genoppten Gummiteppich ausgelegt ist, befinden sich zwei einander gegenüberliegende Vitrinen, deren eine an den einzigen Stützpfeiler der Gesamtkonstruktion anschließt. Die von zwei Seiten einsichtigen Vitrinen bestehen aus poliertem Stahlblech und fügen sich in eine Gesamtkonstruktion aus Holz mit einem Feinanstrich aus Lackfarbe ein. Das leicht geschwungene Vordach ist auf dieselbe Weise gebaut und gestrichen. Seine Unterseite verlängert die Decke der Halle nach außen. Auf die Flügel der Eingangstüre ist ein graphisches Symbol aufgemalt, das sich in Form von aufgesetzten Metallbändern auf dem Vordach wiederholt und die ebenfalls aus Metall bestehenden Buchstaben einrahmt. Das Ganze ist in enger Harmonie mit der Architektur des Hauses gestaltet.

This uncompromisingly modern design for a fashion shop perfectly sets off the severe beauty of the façade of the eighteenth-century house the shop occupies. Two display windows (one flanked by the only pillar of the overall construction) face each other across a small, raised (two steps) entrance bay floored with grooved rubber matting. Visible from two sides and built of polished sheet steel, they are set in a framing structure of wood finished with gloss paint. The bowed canopy is constructed and finished in the same manner. Its lower face forms an extension of the ceiling of the entrance bay or vestibule. The device painted on the leaves of the door is repeated in metal strips on the front face of the canopy, where it frames the name of the shop, likewise executed in strip metal. The whole composition harmonizes closely with the architecture of the building.

| | | | | | |
|---|---|---|---|---|---|
| Longueur de la façade | 7 m | Fassadenlänge | 7 m | Frontage | 7 m |
| Hauteur | 4,20 m | Höhe | 4,20 m | Height | 4.20 m |
| Profondeur du hall | 2 m | Tiefe der Halle | 2 m | Depth of vestibule | 2 m |

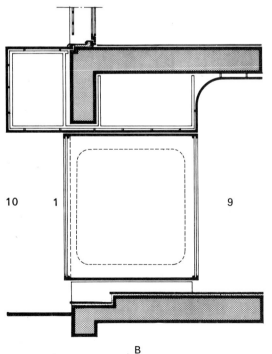

1 2 3 4 m

4 8 12 f

10        1                          9

B

1. Vue générale

1. Gesamtansicht

1. View of the whole shop front

1

5

La maison en briques sombres qui abrite ce magasin d'équipement de cuisines est très belle, mais austère. Aussi, la façade du magasin y apporte une note de fraîcheur et de gaieté très salutaire. La composition caractéristique est issue de l'octogone. La grande vitrine et la porte s'inscrivent dans une construction très épaisse réalisée en menuiserie et habillée de lamifié blanc. Les épaisseurs de l'huisserie ainsi créée sont revêtues de part et d'autre de la glace par un champ plat en aluminium satiné. La porte, dont la poignée est en bois, est cernée d'un bandeau en altuglas coloré équipé de rampes fluorescentes. L'imposte fixe qui éclaire la mezzanine en partie supérieure n'est constituée que d'une grande glace épousant la forme de l'arcade d'origine. Cette glace est posée dans un fin profilé d'aluminium.
Le graphisme et le nom de la firme sont découpés dans un caisson en bois laqué et doublés de plexiglas opaque. Ce caisson, dont l'intérieur est équipé de rampes fluorescentes, est posé en saillie sur la façade de l'immeuble.

Das dunkle Backsteingebäude, in dem dieses Fachgeschäft für Kücheneinrichtungen liegt, zeigt eine sehr schöne, doch strenge Architektur. Die Ladenfassade bringt daher eine wohltuend frische und heitere Note in das Gesamtbild. Die Komposition beruht auf einem Achteck. Das große Schaufenster und die Eingangstüre sind in eine kräftige Holzkonstruktion eingesetzt, die mit weißer Folie verkleidet ist. Die Innenseiten des so geschaffenen Rahmens sind rund um die Glasfläche mit einer flachen Leiste aus mattglänzendem Aluminium verkleidet. Die mit einem Holzgriff versehene Eingangstüre wird von einem Band aus farbigem Glas eingefaßt, das mit Leuchtstoffröhren ausgerüstet ist. Das festeingebaute Oberlicht, durch das der obere Bereich des Zwischengeschosses beleuchtet wird, besteht aus einer einzigen großen Glasscheibe, die der Form der ursprünglichen Arkade angepaßt und in ein dünnes Formblech aus Aluminium eingesetzt ist.
Das Firmensignet und der Firmenname sind auf undurchsichtiges Plexiglas aufgesetzt und in einen Kasten aus lackiertem Holz eingelassen, der sich von der Fassade abhebt. In seinem Inneren befinden sich Leuchtstoffröhren.

The dark-brick building housing this kitchen-equipment shop is extremely fine but somewhat forbidding in appearance, so that the shop front adds a very welcome note of freshness and gaiety. Its distinctive composition is derived from the octagon. The large display window and the door are set in a deep wooden structure clad with white laminated plastic. The inside face of the window aperture on both sides of the glass is clad with sheet aluminium with a satin finish. The door, equipped with a wooden handle, is framed in a strip of coloured altuglass fitted with fluorescent lamps. The fixed fanlight lighting the mezzanine consists of a single large pane of glass filling the shape of the original arch and held in a thin aluminium frame.
The device and the name of the firm are cut out and backed with opaque plexiglass in a painted wooden box projecting from the façade of the building and also containing fluorescent lamps.

| | | | |
|---|---|---|---|
| Longueur de la façade | 5,40 m | Fassadenlänge | 5,40 m |
| Hauteur | 5 m | Höhe | 5 m |

| | |
|---|---|
| Frontage | 5.40 m |
| Height | 5 m |

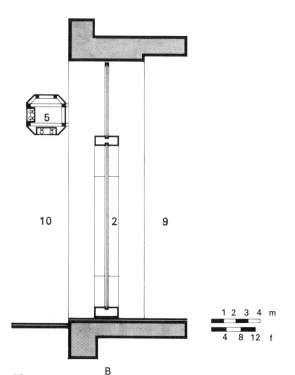

1

2

3

1. Vue générale
2. Le bandeau supérieur
3. La poignée de la porte

1. Gesamtansicht
2. Die Fassadenblende
3. Der Türgriff

1. View of the whole shop front
2. The upper facia
3. The door-handle

4. L'angle de la vitrine et de la porte, et la boîte aux lettres en aluminium
5. Perspective de la vitrine

4. Der Winkel zwischen Schaufenster und Eingangstüre und der Briefkasten aus Aluminium
5. Fluchtlinie des Schaufensters

4. A corner of the window and of the door, showing the aluminium letter-box
5. Another view of the display window

Destiné à un opticien, ce magasin offre une façade entièrement réalisée en acier inoxydable satiné, exception faite des vitrines. Afin d'éviter la monotonie, les parties pleines encadrant la porte et la vitrine sont obliques, accrochant ainsi la lumière différemment. La surface complète de la composition est quadrillée par un jeu de profilés. Chaque carré du damier est rempli, pour les pleins par une plaque métallique dressée sur un panneau de latté, pour les vitrines par une glace claire.

La bande de sol visible devant la vitrine et la porte est en grès cérame, comme le sol de l'intérieur du magasin.

La façade comporte deux enseignes, l'une perpendiculaire, réalisée en plexiglas dans un cadre en métal, l'autre au-dessus de la vitrine, composée de lettres entièrement en plexiglas avec éclairage intérieur.

Die Fassade dieses Optikerfachgeschäfts besteht mit Ausnahme der Schaufenster ganz aus rostfreiem, mattglänzendem Aluminium. Um den Eindruck der Einförmigkeit zu vermeiden, wurden die um die Eingangstüre und das Schaufenster liegenden Massivteile schräg eingesetzt, so daß das Licht unter verschiedenen Winkeln auffällt. Die gesamte Oberfläche der Fassade ist durch Profilleisten in Rechtecke unterteilt. Jedes Quadrat des Schachbretts ist ausgefüllt — die kompakten Partien mit einer auf eine Gitterschablone aufgesetzten Metallplatte, die Vitrinen mit einer durchsichtigen Glasscheibe.

Der vor dem Schaufenster und der Türe sichtbare Fußbodenstreifen besteht, wie der Boden im Ladeninneren, aus Steinfliesen.

Die Ladenfassade weist zwei Beschilderungen auf: Die eine befindet sich im rechten Winkel zur Wand und besteht aus Plexiglas in einem Metallrahmen; die andere setzt sich aus Buchstaben zusammen, die ganz aus Plexiglas hergestellt und mit einer Innenbeleuchtung ausgestattet sind.

This composition, fronting an optician's, is with the exception of the display window executed entirely in satin-finished stainless steel. In order to avoid monotony the solid portions flanking door and window are set at an angle, so that they reflect the light differently. The whole shop front is criss-crossed with sectional members, the solid squares being filled with sheet metal mounted on battened panels and the window squares with clear glass.

The strip of floor in front of window and door is done in the same stoneware as the floor inside the shop.

There are two signs, one at right angles to the shop front and executed in plexiglass with a metal mount, the other consisting of large plexiglass letters lit from inside.

| | | | | | |
|---|---|---|---|---|---|
| Longueur de la façade | 5,80 m | Fassadenlänge | 5,80 m | Frontage | 5.80 m |
| Hauteur | 4,30 m | Höhe | 4,30 m | Height | 4.30 m |

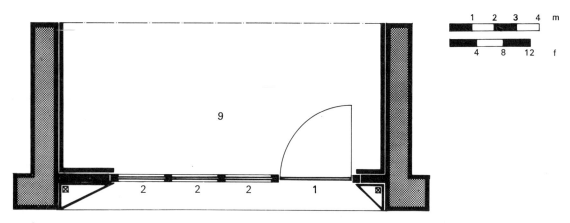

1

2

1. La façade complète
2. Le quadrillage métallique divisant la vitrine
3. La boîte aux lettres dans un des pans coupés latéraux

1. Gesamtansicht der Fassade
2. Die quadratische Metallstruktur der Vitrine
3. Der Briefkastenschlitz in einem der schrägen, seitlichen Fassadenelemente

1. View of the whole shop front
2. Detail of the squared window frame
3. The letter-box in one of the oblique faces

3

Des locaux mitoyens situés à la base de deux maisons anciennes ont permis d'installer un magasin d'accessoires de couture et de travaux d'aiguilles.

Un large pilier de soutènement traité en brique naturelle sépare les deux façades dont une seule est illustrée ici. Bien que les hauteurs disponibles soient différentes, la composition générale respecte le principe d'une division verticale. Des glaces claires alternent avec de petits poteaux formant les huisseries latérales et faisant office de soutènements intermédiaires. La porte d'entrée s'inscrit entre deux de ces petits poteaux. Ces derniers et les poutres supérieures sont laqués; la marche comme le sol du magasin sont en pierre naturelle. La seule signalisation visible est peinte sur les glaces. La voie piétonne sur laquelle s'ouvre ce magasin étant largement éclairée, il n'existe aucune lampe ni aucun spot à l'extérieur.

Im Erdgeschoß zweier alter Häuser wurde in nebeneinanderliegenden Räumen ein Laden für Kurzwaren und Handarbeiten eingerichtet.

Ein großer, in Naturbackstein ausgeführter Stützpfeiler trennt die beiden Fassaden, von denen nur eine hier abgebildet ist. Obwohl die vorliegenden Höhenmaße voneinander abweichen, ist die Gesamtkonzeption nach einem vertikalen Gliederungsprinzip ausgerichtet. Die Fassadenfront zeigt abwechselnd Schaufensterglas und kleine Pfosten, die zugleich als seitliche Einfassung und als Stützelemente dienen. Die Eingangstüre wird von zweien dieser Pfosten eingerahmt. Die Pfosten und die oberen Balken sind lackiert. Die Treppenstufen wie auch der Fußboden im Laden bestehen aus Naturstein.

Die einzig sichtbare Beschilderung ist auf das Schaufenster aufgemalt. Da der Gehsteig vor diesem Laden hell beleuchtet ist, konnte auf Lampen und Spots im Außenbereich verzichtet werden.

Adjacent premises on the ground floors of two old buildings have been converted to house this dressmaking and needlework accessories shop.

The two shop fronts (only one of which is shown here) are separated by a broad supporting pillar faced with natural brick. Although the premises are of different heights the overall composition respects the principle of vertical division. Panes of clear glass alternate with slim uprights that serve both as frames and as intermediate supports. Two of these uprights flank the door. They and the beams above are painted. The outside step and the floor of the shop are of natural stone.

The only sign is painted on the glass. Situated as it is in a very well-lit pedestrian street, the shop has no outside lighting.

| Longueur de la façade | 5 m |
| Hauteur | 3,30 m |

| Fassadenlänge | 5 m |
| Höhe | 3,30 m |

| Frontage | 5 m |
| Height | 3.30 m |

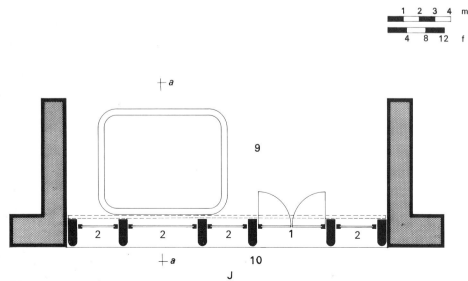

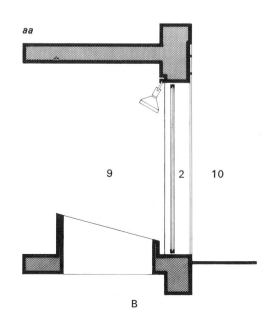

1. La façade la plus large
2. La façade et la maison; à droite, la façade voisine
3. La boîte aux lettres; le cadre en pierres s'inscrit dans la brique

1. Die breitere Fassade
2. Fassade und Haus, rechts die Nachbarfassade
3. Der Briefkasten; die Steineinfassung fügt sich in den umgebenden Backstein ein

1. The wider of the two shop fronts
2. View of the façade of the building, showing part of the other shop front on the right
3. The letter-box; its stone surround is let into the brickwork

## 15.   Blizzard, Copenhagen          Leif Wolfsberg, Arch., Copenhagen

La façade de ce magasin de vêtements est très attrayante et dynamique. Elle est réalisée dans un matériau économique: le bois (massif et contre-plaqué sur armature en menuiserie). La qualité de la peinture laquée assure une unité très réussie. Les deux piliers latéraux encadrant la vitrine montent sur toute la hauteur de la composition. En partie supé-rieure, le bandeau qui sépare ces piliers est habillé par un alignement de cylindres verticaux sur lesquels a été peint un graphisme aux couleurs vives. L'entrée du magasin se trouve dans une galerie couverte perpendiculaire à la vitrine exté-rieure. Le seuil de la porte d'entrée se prolonge devant la vitrine; il est en carreaux de céramique.
La signalisation peinte sur la traverse longeant le bandeau et sur les volumes fixés aux piliers est éclairée par une série de spots orientables. Ceux-ci sont groupés dans des cylindres métalliques laqués, fixés latéralement, en nette avancée par rapport à la façade. Ces cylindres supportent eux aussi une signalisation lisible verticalement.

Die Fassade dieses Bekleidungsgeschäfts wirkt sehr anziehend in ihrer Dynamik. Es wurde dafür kostensparendes Material verwendet, Massivholz und Holzfurnier auf Sperrholzunterlage. Die Quali-tät des Lackanstrichs gewährleistet ein gelungenes einheitliches Aussehen. Die beiden das Schaufen-ster einrahmenden Seitenpfeiler nehmen die ganze Höhe der Komposition ein. Die breite, die beiden Pfeiler trennende Fassadenblende im oberen Teil ist mit einer Reihe vertikaler Zylinder verkleidet, auf die in kräftigen Farben ein graphisches Design aufge-malt ist. Der Ladeneingang befindet sich in einer überdachten Galerie, die im rechten Winkel zur äußeren Schaufensterauslage liegt. Die Schwelle der Eingangstüre ist bis vor das Schaufenster vor-gezogen und besteht aus keramischen Fliesen.
Die Ladenbeschilderung, die auf den Querbalken entlang der Fassadenblende und auf die an den Pfeilern angebrachten Elemente aufgemalt ist, wird von einer Reihe verstellbarer Spots angestrahlt, die in seitlich vor der Fassadenlinie montierte Zylinder aus lackiertem Metall eingebaut sind. Diese Zylin-der tragen selbst auch eine Beschriftung, die senk-recht vor oben nach unten gelesen wird.

This clothing shop has an extremely attractive and dynamic front. It is executed in inexpensive materials—timber and plywood mounted on woo-den frameworks. The quality of the gloss-paint finish successfully draws the composition togeth-er. The two pillars flanking the display window run the whole height of the shop front. The broad facia above the display window and between the pillars is made up of a row of vertical cylinders with a brightly-coloured device painted on them. Entrance is by way of a covered gallery at right angles to the outside display window. The door-step, which extends along the front of the display window, is of ceramic tile.
The name painted on the bottom band of the facia and the initials painted on the volumes attached to the pillars are lit by a series of movable spots housed in enamelled-metal cylinders held on brackets at either side of, and projecting some way out from, the shop front. The cylinders also bear a further sign that reads vertically.

| | | | |
|---|---|---|---|
| Longueur de la façade | 4,60 m | Fassadenlänge | 4,60 m |
| Hauteur | 4,20 m | Höhe | 4,20 m |

| | |
|---|---|
| Frontage | 4.60 m |
| Height | 4.20 m |

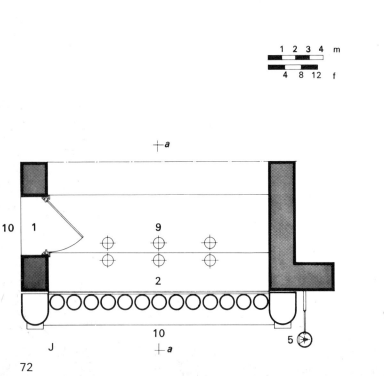

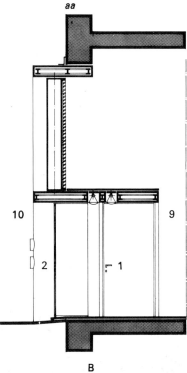

1. Un angle de la vitrine

1. Eine Ecke der Auslage

1. A corner of the display window

3

2

2. Le bandeau supérieur
3. Un cylindre d'éclairage
4. La façade dans sa totalité

2. Die Fassadenblende
3. Ein Zylinder mit Beleuchtungskörpern
4. Gesamtansicht der Fassade

2. Detail of the upper part of the shop front
3. One of the lighting cylinders
4. View of the whole shop front

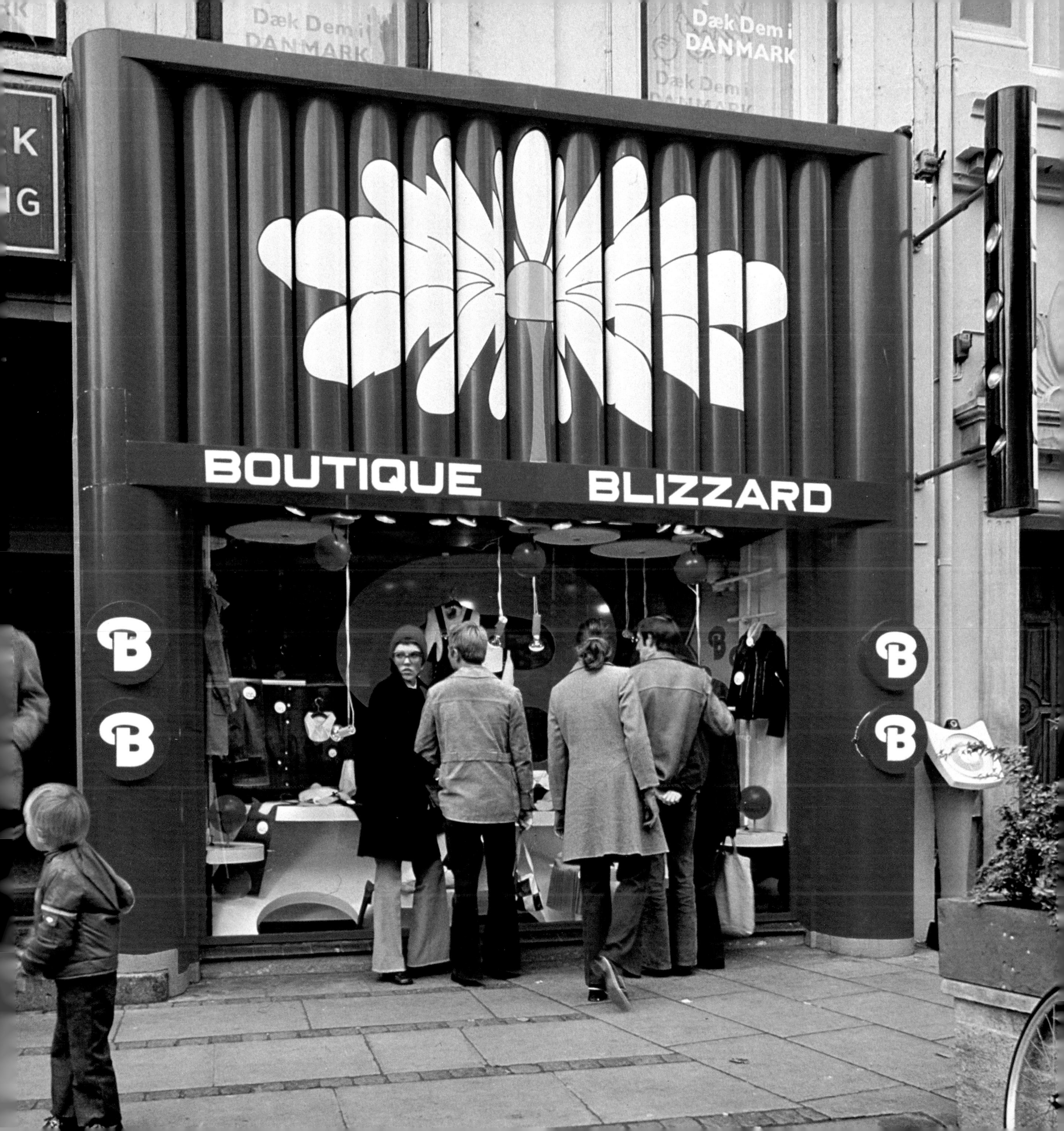
Dæk Dem i
DANMARK
BOUTIQUE
BLIZZARD
B
B
B
B

## 16. Galerie Hoeppner, München — Peter Lanz, Arch., München

Cette devanture est aussi un mur-cloison séparant la galerie-café de l'extérieur. En effet, le local est installé dans un ensemble contemporain où alternent des galeries couvertes, des cours en plein air, des plates-formes pour la promenade et le shopping. Ainsi le public peut faire le tour complet de la galerie. Le mur de «ceinture» est réalisé par la juxtaposition (avec de larges joints creux) de modules industrialisés en tôle laquée, fixés sur un cadre en bois et métal, et intérieurement doublés. Les huisseries des diverses parties vitrées (également modulées) toute hauteur, ainsi que celles des impostes sont en bois teinté. Le sas d'entrée, en avancée sur l'une des façades, accroche le regard. Sur sa partie extérieure en glace claire se détache une signalisation peinte. Entre les deux portes de ce sas, toute la surface du sol est habillée d'un épais tapis-brosse.

Diese Auslage hat zugleich die Funktion einer Trennwand, die Galerie und Café nach außen abschirmt. Das Lokal liegt in einem modernen Komplex, in dem überdachte Galerien, freie Höfe und Innenterrassen für den Einkaufsbummel miteinander abwechseln. Das Publikum kann so um die ganze Galerie herumschlendern. Die äußere «Ringmauer» setzt sich aus vorgefertigten Modulen aus lackiertem Blech zusammen, die unter Freilassung breiter Schlitze aneinandergefügt und auf einen aus Holz und Metall bestehend Rahmen aufmontiert sind; ihre Innenseite ist verkleidet. Die Rahmen der verschiedenen, in voller Höhe verglasten Flächen (ebenfalls Module), sowie die Rahmen der Oberlichter bestehen aus eingefärbtem Holz. Die einer der Fassadenfronten vorgelagerte Eingangszone zieht den Blick auf sich; auf der aus durchsichtigem Glas bestehenden Außenfläche ist eine Beschriftung angebracht. Der Fußboden zwischen den beiden Türen der Eingangszone ist mit einer dicken Matte ausgelegt.

This shop front is at the same time a partition wall separating the gallery/café from the outside. The premises form part of a modern complex with alternating covered galleries, open-air courts, and promenade and shopping levels. People can in fact walk all round the gallery. The enclosing wall is made of prefabricated enamelled-metal elements (with broad, open jointing) secured to a wood-and-metal framework and lined inside. The frames of the various full-height glazed portions (also prefabricated elements) as well as those of the transom windows are of stained wood. A vestibule projects from one of the fronts, catching the eye, and on the outside of it there is a sign painted on clear glass. The entire floor surface between the two doors of the vestibule is covered with a large, thick doormat.

| Longueur de la façade | 75 m | Fassadenlänge | 75 m | Frontage | 75 m |
|---|---|---|---|---|---|
| Hauteur | 2,80 m | Höhe | 2,80 m | Height | 2.80 m |
| Profondeur du sas | 1,50 m | Tiefe der Eingangszone | 1,50 m | Depth of vestibule | 1.50 m |

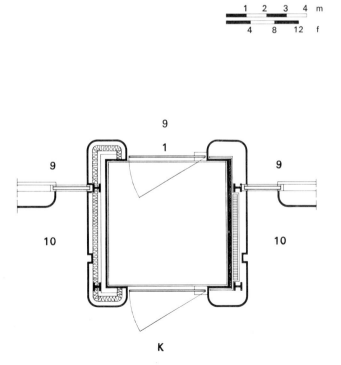

K

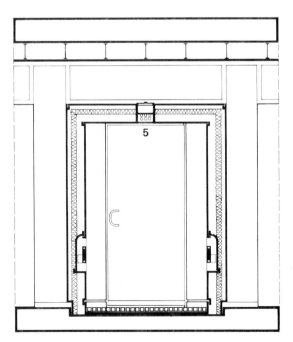

H

1. Une partie de la galerie côté patio

1. Teilansicht der Galerie auf der Seite des Innenhofs

1. Part of the gallery, seen from the patio side

2. Le sas d'entrée et, en arrière-plan, une des vitrines
3. Les impostes et le bandeau en béton de la dalle supérieure
4. Un angle cerné de deux joints creux
5. Le sas d'entrée et le passage couvert ceinturant la la galerie

2. Die Eingangszone, im Hintergrund eine der Auslagen
3. Die Oberlichter und die Betonfront der oberen Fassadenblende
4. Ecke der Ringmauer mit zwei offenen Schlitzen
5. Die Eingangszone und der überdachte Umgang um die Galerie

2. The vestibule, with one of the display windows in the background
3. The transom windows and the concrete moulding of the upper level
4. Detail of a corner, showing two of the open joints
5. The entrance vestibule and the covered passage round the gallery

2

3

4

Galerie
Cafe
Hans Hoeppner

La façade de cette bijouterie est réalisée en plastique moulé fixé sur une armature en bois. Les vitrines en aluminium mat sont situées très en retrait du large bandeau supérieur. Ainsi la lumière naturelle, parfois trop violente et peu flatteuse, est atténuée considérablement, et les bijoux sont présentés sous une lumière étudiée et dirigée avec soin. Cet effet d'écrin lumineux dans l'ombre est encore accentué par le vide préservé sous les vitrines situées à un mètre du sol. Le sol de la mini-galerie couverte, en dalle de granit, se prolonge au fond de ces niches ouvertes de part et d'autre de la porte centrale en glace. Une boule d'acier chromé y tient lieu de poignée.
Les lettres formant le nom du magasin sont réalisées en tôle d'acier. Elles contiennent un tube néon qui, la nuit venue, crée un halo lumineux très subtil, ne luttant pas avec la brillance de la présentation. Il en est de même de l'éclairage d'ambiance assuré par quelques spots encastrés dans la construction.

Die Fassade dieses Juweliergeschäfts besteht aus gegossenem Plastikmaterial, das auf eine Holzunterlage montiert ist. Die Vitrinen aus mattem Aluminium sind deutlich hinter die obere Fassadenblende zurückgesetzt. Dadurch wird das manchmal zu grelle und ungünstige Tageslicht merklich abgeschwächt, und der Schmuck kann unter einer sorgfältig überlegten und gezielten Beleuchtung ausgestellt werden. Der Eindruck einer beleuchteten Leinwand im Dunkeln wird durch den Hohlraum unterhalb der Vitrinen, die einen Meter über dem Boden liegen, noch verstärkt. Der aus Granitplatten bestehende Bodenbelag der kleinen überdachten Galerie setzt sich bis in diese offenen Nischen zu beiden Seiten der zentralen Glaseingangstüre fort. Eine Kugel aus verchromtem Stahl dient als Türgriff.
Die Buchstaben des Firmenschilds bestehen aus Stahlblech. Sie sind mit einer Neonröhre ausgerüstet, deren sanfter Lichtschein nachts den Glanz der Auslagen nicht beeinträchtigt. Die gleiche Wirkung erreicht die allgemeine Beleuchtung, die durch eingebaute Spots erfolgt.

The front of this jeweller's shop is executed in moulded plastic secured to a wooden framework. The matt-finish aluminium windows are deeply set back beneath the broad facia. This cuts out quite a lot of daylight, which can be harsh and unflattering, and means that the jewellery can be displayed in carefully controlled lighting. The effect of a luminous casket suspended in darkness is further increased by the gap beneath the windows, which start a metre up from the ground. The granite-paved floor of the shallow gallery thus extends beneath the windows on either side of the central glass door. The door-handle is a ball of chromium-plated steel.
The lettering of the name is done in sheet steel with neon tubing inside, which at night creates a delicate halo of light that in no way conflicts with the brilliance of the window display. The same is true of the ambient lighting provided by a number of sunken spots.

| Longueur de la façade | 4,40 m | Fassadenlänge | 4,40 m | Frontage | 4.40 m |
| Hauteur | 3,60 m | Höhe | 3,60 m | Height | 3.60 m |

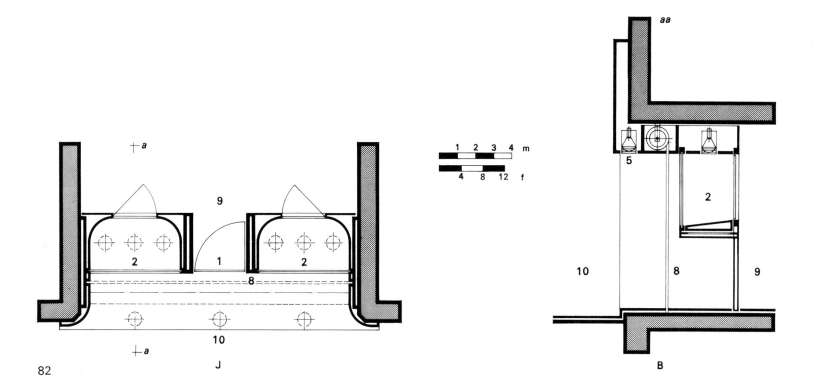

1. Vue frontale du magasin
2. Les vitrines et la porte d'entrée
3. Vue frontale d'une des vitrines
4. La façade et ses deux enseignes

1. Frontalansicht des Geschäfts
2. Die Vitrinen und die Eingangstüre
3. Frontalansicht einer Vitrine
4. Die Fassade mit den zwei Firmen-
   schildern

1. View of the whole shop front
2. The display windows and the entrance
3. Front view of one of the display
   windows
4. General view of the shop front,
   showing the two signs

Ce vaste magasin de chaussures occupe tout le rez-de-chaussée d'un remarquable immeuble dont la paroi extérieure est traitée en tôle d'acier laquée industriellement.

Plusieurs encorbellements surplombent les glaces et les parties pleines séparant le magasin de la cour-patio aux divers emmarchements. Certaines vitrines occupent toute la hauteur disponible, d'autres se présentent comme de longues bandes à 1,30 m du sol et permettent une présentation des produits plus élaborée et plus intimiste. Dans ces dernières vitrines, la sous-face oblique de l'encorbellement inférieur se prolonge franchement. Des spots directionnels s'y trouvent encastrés. Deux portes d'entrée sont inscrites dans les glaces toute hauteur. Leurs poignées sont en métal laqué. Le même matériau constitue les lettres en relief de la raison sociale placée sur une partie pleine à la hauteur du regard.

Dieses große Schuhgeschäft nimmt das ganze Erdgeschoß eines interessanten Gebäudes ein, dessen Außenwand in industriemäßig lackiertem Stahlblech ausgeführt ist.

Mehrere Vorsprünge überlagern die Front der Schaufenster und kompakten Flächen, durch die der Verkaufsraum von dem durch mehrere Treppen gegliederten Innenhof abgetrennt ist. Einige Auslagen nehmen die ganze verfügbare Höhe ein, andere ziehen sich wie lange Bänder in etwa 1,30 Meter Abstand vom Boden hin und ermöglichen eine durchdachte und persönlicher gestaltete Ausstellung der Ware. Die abgeschrägte Unterseite des untersten Mauervorsprungs setzt sich bis in diese letztgenannten Vitrinen hinein fort. In diese schräge Fläche sind mehrere Spots eingebaut. In die in ganzer Höhe durchgehenden Schaufenster sind zwei Eingangstüren eingefügt. Die Türgriffe bestehen aus lackiertem Metall. Dasselbe Material wurde für die plastisch aufgesetzten Buchstaben des Firmennamens verwendet, der auf einer in Blickhöhe liegenden Wandfläche angebracht ist.

This large shoe shop occupies the entire ground floor of a remarkable building of which the outside wall is clad with industrially enamelled sheet steel.

There are a number of overhangs above the windows and solid portions separating the shop from the courtyard with its different levels. Some of the windows occupy the whole height of the front; others are in the form of long strips set 1.30 m from the ground and permitting a more intimate and elaborate display of goods. In the strip windows the oblique underface of the lower overhang is boldly extended and has movable spots sunk in it. There are two doors in the full-length windows. The handles are of enamelled metal, the same material being used for the lettering of the name, which stands out in relief at eye-level on one of the solid portions of the shop front.

| Longueur de la façade | 19 m |
|---|---|
| Hauteurs | 4,80/2,60 m |

| Fassadenlänge | 19 m |
|---|---|
| Höhenmaße | 4,80/2,60 m |

| Frontage | 19 m |
|---|---|
| Heights | 4.80/2.60 m |

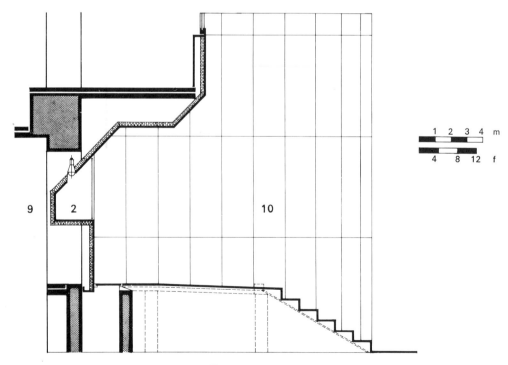

B

2

3

2. Les grandes vitrines au centre; à gauche, la vitrine étroite
3. La perspective de la façade
4. Un détail de la façade; au premier plan, la vitrine étroite reflétant l'architecture extérieure

2. Die großen Vitrinen in der Mitte, links die schmale Vitrine
3. Fluchtlinie der Fassade
4. Detail der Fassade, im Vordergrund die schmale Vitrine, in der sich die Architektur des Außenbereichs spiegelt

2. The large centre windows, with a strip window on the left
3. View along the front
4. A detail of the shop front, with the strip window in the foreground reflecting a part of the surrounding architecture

Ce vaste magasin d'alimentation occupe toute la surface au sol d'un immeuble contemporain. La façade proprement dite est rythmée par les larges huisseries en bois teinté encadrant les glaces claires des vitrines et les deux portes d'entrée situées à une extrémité.
La largeur constante entre les huisseries a déterminé le dessin des ondulations d'une marquise longeant toute la composition. Cette marquise est réalisée en fibre de verre avec durcisseur coloré possédant un faible coefficient de dilatation. La construction, bien que fort robuste, est très légère; les panneaux préformés ont été vissés et collés sur une armature en serrurerie. Les eaux pluviales sont canalisées à chaque extrémité de la marquise. Chacune des vagues inférieures de celle-ci est équipée d'un éclairage fluorescent encastré.

Dieses große Lebensmittelgeschäft nimmt das ganze Erdgeschoß eines modernen Gebäudes ein. Die Geschäftsfassade ist durch große Rahmen aus eingefärbtem Holz rhythmisch untergliedert, in die die Glasscheiben der Auslagen und die beiden, am äußeren Ende einer Seite liegenden Eingangstüren eingesetzt sind.
Die konstante Breite zwischen den Rahmen war bestimmend für das wellenförmige Design eines Vordaches, das die ganze Fassade entlangläuft. Dieses Vordach besteht aus Glasfiber mit einem durchgefärbten Härter, der einen schwachen Ausdehnungskoeffizienten besitzt. Die Konstruktion ist trotz ihrer Robustheit sehr leicht; die vorgefertigten Platten wurden miteinander verschraubt und auf einem geschlossenen Gestell befestigt. Das Regenwasser wird an den Außenseiten des Vordaches aufgefangen. An den Wellentälern des Vordaches ist jeweils eine Beleuchtung aus Leuchtstoffröhren angebracht.

This vast food shop occupies the entire ground floor of a modern building. The shop front proper is treated rhythmically with broad frames of stained wood enclosing the clear glass of the windows and the two doors situated at one end.
The constant distance between the uprights dictated the undulations of the canopy that runs along the whole front. The canopy is executed in fibreglass with a coloured hardening agent that has a low coefficient of expansion. This very solid yet at the same time extremely light construction is made up of prefabricated panels bolted and glued to a metal framework. Rainwater is run down at either end of the canopy. Each convex curve on the underside is fitted with a sunken fluorescent lamp.

| Longueur de la façade | 15,50 m | Fassadenlänge | 15,50 m | Frontage | 15.50 m |
| Hauteur | 3,10 m | Höhe | 3,10 m | Height | 3.10 m |

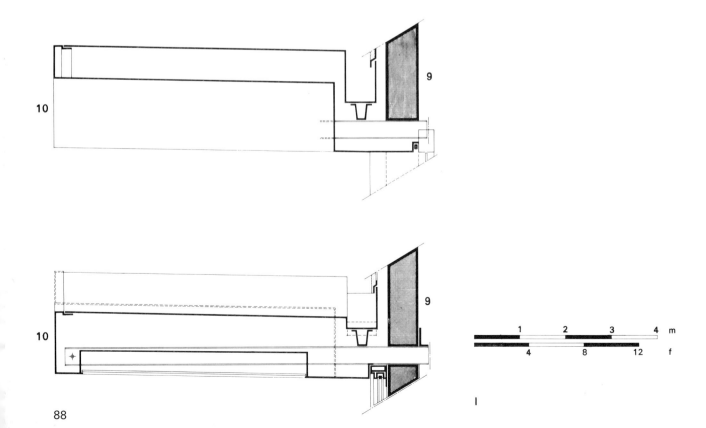

1. Les ondulations de la marquise et les bandes de lumière

1. Die Wellenlinien des Vordaches und die eingebauten Lichtbänder

1. The undulating canopy, showing the fluorescent strips

1

2. Les poignées des portes d'entrée
3. La marquise surplombant les vitrines et les portes d'entrée

2. Die Handgriffe der Eingangstüren
3. Das Vordach über den Schaufenstern und den Eingangstüren

2. The door-handles
3. The canopy overhanging the display windows and the doors

2

Ce magasin proposant du matériel de haute fidélité est installé à la base d'un immeuble très caractéristique par son alternance de bandes claires et foncées.
La plus grande partie du rez-de-chaussée est utilisée par un magasin de vêtements masculins. La galerie HI-FI n'occupe qu'une faible surface. Elle communique avec la rue par une vaste glace teintée groupant la vitrine proprement dite et la porte d'entrée. Le graphisme est réalisé en métal collé directement sur la glace. Cette ouverture aux angles arrondis est cernée d'un épais profilé en acier inoxydable qui se prolonge latéralement. Toutes les autres vitrines et portes du magasin voisin sont traitées de la même manière. La façade, dans sa totalité, est réalisée en marbre blanc sous forme d'un parement en plaques rectangulaires. L'éclairage extérieur est assuré par des appliques en métal et verre dépoli qui se répartissent régulièrement.

Dieses High Fidelity-Fachgeschäft liegt im Erdgeschoß eines Gebäudes, das durch den Wechsel heller und dunkler Gesimsbänder ein charakteristisches Aussehen gewinnt.
Den größeren Teil des Erdgeschosses nimmt ein Geschäft für Herrenbekleidung ein. Der Hi-Fi Galerie steht nur eine sehr kleine Fläche zur Verfügung. Die Verbindung zur Straße stellt eine große farbige Glasscheibe her, die in Auslage und Eingangstüre unterteilt ist. Die Beschriftung besteht aus Metallbuchstaben, die direkt auf das Glas aufgeklebt sind.
Die mit abgerundeten Ecken versehene Maueröffnung wird von einem starken Profilblech aus nichtrostendem Stahl eingefaßt, das sich nach außen verbreitert. Sämtliche Auslagen und Türen des benachbarten Geschäfts sind in der gleichen Weise ausgeführt. Die gesamte Fassade ist mit weißem Marmor in Form rechteckiger Platten verkleidet. Für die Außenbeleuchtung sind Lampen aus Metall und matt geschliffenem Glas in regelmäßigen Abständen angebracht.

This high-fidelity equipment shop occupies premises on the ground floor of a building with a distinctive pattern of alternating dark and light bands.
Most of the ground floor is taken up by a men's outfitter's, the 'HIFI Galerie' occupying only a small part. It communicates with the street via a large expanse of tinted plate glass comprising the display window proper and the entrance. The sign is executed in metal stuck straight on the glass. The whole aperture with its rounded corners is framed by a broad stainless-steel section projecting from the façade. The windows and doors of the adjacent shop are treated in the same manner. The façade as a whole is clad with rectangular slabs of white marble. Outside lighting is provided by fittings of metal and frosted glass distributed evenly along the façade.

| Longueur de la vitrine | 4,20 m |
| Hauteur | 2,40 m |

| Schaufensterlänge | 4,20 m |
| Höhe | 2,40 m |

| Length of display window | 4.20 m |
| Height | 2.40 m |

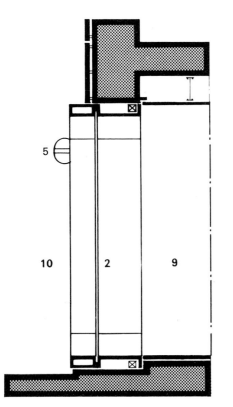

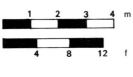

1

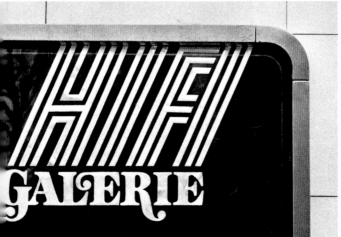

2 3

Ce magasin est un vaste hall où sont présentées des voitures de tourisme. Il s'inscrit à la base d'un immeuble aux proportions rigoureuses. Les volumes caractéristiques à pans coupés qui saillent plus ou moins vers l'extérieur apportent un jeu de brillances, de valeurs et d'ombres qui intriguent le passant.

Le plafond du sas extérieur qui précède l'entrée est constitué par le retour incliné d'un de ces volumes sur lequel se dessine le graphisme lumineux d'une des marques présentées.

Les volumes vitrés donnent jour sur une mezzanine intérieure. Les glaces de la vitrine sont concaves, ce qui évite les reflets. Il est à noter que le jeu des pans coupés extérieurs se retrouve à l'intérieur assurant à l'ensemble une belle unité. Le métal laqué satiné ou brillant (cadre coloré de la vitrine) est le seul matériau opaque utilisé pour cette réalisation. Les autres matériaux employés sont le verre armé et la glace claire.

Dieser Geschäftsraum ist eine große Ausstellungshalle für Personenkraftwagen. Er liegt im Erdgeschoß eines Gebäudes mit strengen Proportionen. Charakteristische Elemente mit abgeschrägten Flächen, die mehr oder weniger stark nach außen vorspringen, erzeugen ein Wechselspiel von Lichteffekten und Hell-Dunkel-Abstufungen, das die Aufmerksamkeit der Passanten auf sich zieht.

Die Decke der dem Eingang vorgelagerten Außenzone wird von der geneigten Unterseite eines dieser Elemente gebildet, auf dem das Markenzeichen einer der austellenden Firmen in Leuchtschrift angebracht ist.

Durch die verglasten Teile fällt Licht auf das Zwischengeschoß im Inneren. Die Scheiben der Vitrine sind konkav geschliffen, so daß Spiegelungen vermieden werden. Bemerkenswert ist die Wiederholung der abgeschrägten Elemente des Außenbereichs im Inneren, wodurch die Anlage wohltuend einheitlich wirkt. Neben armiertem Glas und Schaufensterglas wurde in dieser Komposition als einziges undurchsichtiges Material Metall in seidenmatter oder glänzender Lackierung (farbiger Rahmen der Vitrine) verwendet.

This large car showroom occupies premises on the ground floor of a building of rigorous design. Distinctive volumes made up of canted surfaces project in varying degrees and capture the attention of passers-by with their intriguing play of light and shade.

The ceiling of the vestibule leading to the entrance is formed of the inclined underside of one of these volumes and bears the illuminated device of one of the makes displayed.

The glazed volumes light an inside mezzanine. The panes of the display window are concave in order to avoid reflection. A notable feature is that the play of canted surfaces on the outside is taken up again inside the showroom, giving a splendid unity to the whole design. Satin- or gloss-finish enamelled metal (the coloured frame of the display window) is the only opaque material used here, the other materials being clear and reinforced glass.

| Longueur de la façade | 11,70 m |
|---|---|
| Hauteur | 5,50 m |
| Profondeur du sas | 3 m |

| Fassadenlänge | 11,70 m |
|---|---|
| Höhe | 5,50 m |
| Tiefe der Eingangszone | 3 m |

| Frontage | 11.70 m |
|---|---|
| Height | 5.50 m |
| Depth of vestibule | 3 m |

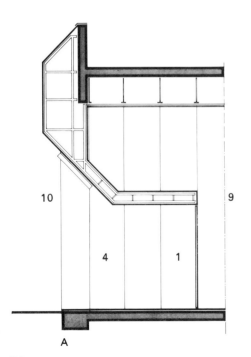

A

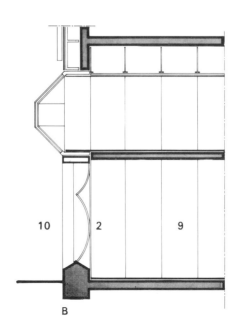

B

1.   La vitrine et ses glaces concaves

1.   Die Vitrine mit den konkaven Schaufensterscheiben

1.   The concave panes of the display window

3

4

5

Cette boutique de prêt-à-porter de «luxe» s'inscrit dans une des cellules qui rythment l'architecture inférieure d'un vaste ensemble contemporain.

Le caractère très affirmé de la composition, la répartition générale et impérative des huisseries horizontales et verticales lors des finitions de l'immeuble obligeaient à respecter une unité qu'aurait détruite une composition arbitrairement plaquée. Seul le vaste graphisme de la raison sociale attire et intrigue le passant. Il situe parfaitement la boutique parmi ses voisines de jour comme de nuit, puisqu'il est lumineux. Les trois lettres sont réalisées en tôle laquée avec une face en plexiglas opaque dissimulant des tubes néon. Les matériaux, d'ailleurs identiques pour tous les autres magasins, sont la pierre polie, l'aluminium et la glace. Le sol du petit sas d'entrée est tendu d'un tapis de caoutchouc alvéolé.

Diese Boutique für «Luxuskonfektion» liegt in einer der Zellen, die die untere Architekturzone eines großen Gebäudekomplexes aufgliedern.

Der ausgeprägte Charakter der Anlage, die konsequent durchgeführte Verteilung der waagerechten und senkrechten Rahmen bei der Außengestaltung des Gebäudes, zwang zur Bewahrung einer Einheitlichkeit, die durch eine willkürlich aufgesetzte Ladenfassade zerstört worden wäre. Einzig der große Schriftzug des Firmennamens weckt die Aufmerksamkeit des Passanten. Er hebt die Boutique auch nachts durch die Leuchtschrift deutlich unter den benachbarten Läden heraus. Die drei Buchstaben bestehen aus lackiertem Blech mit einer Front aus undurchsichtigem Plexiglas, hinter der sich Neonröhren verbergen. Die verwendeten Materialien sind dieselben wie bei allen anderen Läden: polierter Stein, Aluminium und Schaufensterglas. Der Fußboden im kleinen Vorraum der Eingangszone ist mit einem wabenförmig strukturierten Gummibelag ausgelegt.

This de luxe ready-to-wear boutique occupies one of the cells making up the lower part of a large modern complex.

The distinctive character of the architecture and the general distribution of the horizontals and verticals that constitute an integral part of the finish of the building dictated respect for a unity that would have been destroyed by an arbitrary composition slapped onto the front. The enormous lettering of the name is all that seeks to capture the eye of the passer-by and attract his or her interest. It picks the boutique out from its neighbours superbly both by day and, since it is luminous, by night. The three letters are executed in enamelled sheet steel with an opaque plexiglass front concealing neon tubing. The other materials used in this and all the other shop fronts in the building are polished stone, aluminium, and plate glass. The small vestibule is floored with grooved rubber matting.

| Longueur de la façade | 4,20 m |
| Hauteur | 6 m |

| Fassadenlänge | 4,20 m |
| Höhe | 6 m |

| Frontage | 4.20 m |
| Height | 6 m |

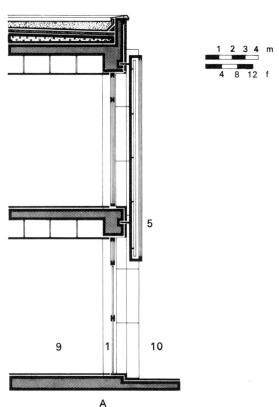

1 2 3 4 m

4 8 12 f

A

1. Vue frontale du magasin et de l'immeuble
2. L'immense signalisation en tôle et en plexiglas
3. La poignée de la porte d'entrée
4. Détail de la partie inférieure du sas

1. Frontalansicht des Ladens und des Gebäudes
2. Die überdimensionale Beschilderung aus Blech und Plexiglas
3. Der Handgriff der Eingangstüre
4. Detail des unteren Bereichs der Eingangszone

1. View of the whole shop front and part of the building
2. The vast sheet-steel and plexiglass sign
3. The door-handle
4. Detail of the lower part of the vestibule

## 23. Kaufhof, Hamburg

Bureau d'étude du magasin / Entwurfsbüro des «Kaufhofes» / The store's design office, Hamburg

Ce grand magasin, installé dans une ancienne construction, occupe la surface de presque tout un quartier. Les nombreux étages sont équipés en surfaces de vente. Les deux côtés du bâtiment orientés vers les artères les plus passantes comportent des galeries couvertes où la promenade est très attrayante, car elles sont bordées du côté intérieur par des vitrines toute hauteur, et du côté extérieur par des blocs de vitrines installés entre les arcades. La structure de ces blocs est réalisée en métal laqué. Les autres matériaux sont la pierre pour le sol et le marbre blanc pour les retombées au-dessus des vitrines toute hauteur; ils s'associent parfaitement à la brique qui reste le matériau dominant.

Le nom du magasin se retrouve régulièrement sur les bandeaux intérieurs de la galerie. Les lettres sont réalisées en métal et en plexiglas; elles comportent un éclairage intérieur. Plusieurs immenses enseignes verticales barrent en outre la façade sur la totalité de l'immeuble.

Dieses große, in einem Altbau eingerichtete Kaufhaus nimmt die Fläche fast eines ganzen Häuserviertels ein. Die zahlreichen Stockwerke sind als Verkaufsflächen ausgebaut. An den beiden Gebäudeseiten, die an den belebtesten Straßenzügen entlangführen, befinden sich überdachte Galerien, die zu einem abwechslungsreichen Schaufensterbummel einladen; die Galerien werden auf der Innenseite von wandhohen Auslagen flankiert, auf der Außenseite von Vitrinenblöcken, die zwischen die Arkaden eingesetzt sind. Das Gerüst dieser Vitrinen besteht aus lackiertem Metall. Weitere Baustoffe sind Stein für den Bodenbelag und weißer Marmor für die Blenden über den wandhohen Auslagen. Beide Materialien passen gut zu dem vorherrschend gebliebenen Backstein.

Der Firmenname des Kaufhauses erscheint in regelmäßigen Abständen an den Blenden innerhalb der Galerie. Die Buchstaben bestehen aus Metall und Plexiglas und sind mit einer Innenbeleuchtung ausgestattet. Darüberhinaus sind auf dem gesamten Gebäude mehrere riesige, senkrecht zur Fassade verlaufende Firmenschilder angebracht.

This large department store in an old building occupies, with its many sales floors, virtually the area of an entire city district. On the two sides of the building facing the busiest streets there are attractive arcades inviting one to stroll along between full-length display windows on the inside and glass display cases between the arches on the outside. The structure of these display cases is executed in enamelled metal. Other materials used are stone for the floor and white marble above the display windows, both of which go very well with the dominant material, which is brick.

The name of the store appears at regular intervals along a band running the length of the arcades, the letters being executed in metal and plexiglass and lit from inside. In addition there is a number of enormous vertical signs running the entire height of the façade.

| | | | | | | |
|---|---|---|---|---|---|---|
| Longueur d'une arcade | 3,50 m | Länge einer Arkade | 3,50 m | Width of arches | 3.50 m |
| Longueur d'une vitrine | 2,20 m | Länge einer Vitrine | 2,20 m | Width of display windows | 2.20 m |
| Hauteur d'une vitrine | 2 m | Höhe einer Vitrine | 2 m | Height of display windows | 2 m |

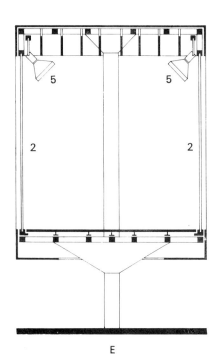

E

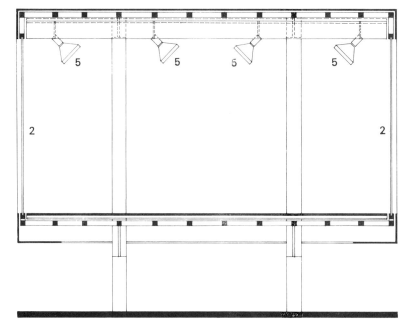

F

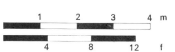

1

1. La galerie couverte et les vitrines intérieures
2. Les vitrines extérieures

1. Die überdachte Galerie und die inneren Auslagen
2. Die äußeren Vitrinen

1. The arcade, showing the inside display windows
2. The outer display cases

2

**4**

**5**

6

A la base de ce vaste immeuble occupant un ancien pâté de maisons, de nombreux commerçants se sont installés dans des locaux présentant le même aspect extérieur. Le couturier a choisi de se placer au bout de la place et à l'angle d'une galerie couverte pénétrant à l'intérieur de la construction. Comme toute la façade de cette dernière, les parties pleines de la façade du magasin sont traitées en tôle d'acier (habillage des piliers cylindriques de soutènement et du bandeau), ou en métal plein (huisseries des vitrines et des portes). La couleur unique est un brun soutenu. Les grandes vitrines toute hauteur se présentent sur deux plans reliés entre eux par des vitrines plus étroites formant des pans coupés. Le sol du magasin est au même niveau que celui du trottoir; toutefois, une large bande de pierre polie crée une rupture salutaire entre les deux endroits.
Sur le bandeau, les lettres formant la raison sociale sont en acier chromé brillant; elles sont éclairées par des spots situés latéralement. Le store-corbeille en toile blanche distingue élégamment le magasin de ses voisins et apporte une douceur bien adaptée à l'activité commerciale.

Im Erdgeschoß dieses Gebäudekomplexes, der einen ganzen alten Häuserblock einnimmt, befinden sich zahlreiche Läden und Geschäfte, die äußerlich alle den gleichen Anblick bieten. Der Inhaber des Modeladens wählte die Lage am Ende des Platzes und am Eck einer überdachten Galerie, die in das Innere des Gebäudes hineinführt. Wie die gesamte Gebäudefassade wurden auch die kompakten Partien der Geschäftsfassade in Stahlblech ausgeführt (Verkleidung der zylindrischen Stützpfeiler und der Fassadenblende) oder in massivem Metall (Rahmen der Auslagen und Türen). Die einzige verwendete Farbe ist ein kräftiges Braun. Die in ganzer Höhe durchgehenden, großen Schaufenster liegen auf zwei Ebenen und sind durch schmälere, schräg eingesetzte Vitrinen miteinander verbunden. Der Fußboden des Ladens liegt auf gleicher Höhe mit dem Gehsteig, doch bewirkt ein breites Band aus poliertem Stein die Trennung der beiden Bereiche.
Die auf der Fassadenblende angebrachten Buchstaben des Firmennamens bestehen aus glanzverchromten Stahl; sie werden von seitlich montierten Spots beleuchtet. Die Markise aus weissem Segeltuch ist ein elegantes Unterscheidungsmerkmal zu den benachbarten Läden und schafft darüberhinaus eine legere Atmosphäre, die dem Geschäftsgang zugute kommt.

Part of the ground floor of this huge building occupying an entire block is devoted to a number of retail business premises all identical in outside appearance. The couturier chose one on a corner between the street facing the square and an arcade running back inside the building. Like the entire façade of the building, the solid portions of the shop front are executed in sheet steel (cladding the supporting columns and the facia) and solid metal (window and door frames). A dignified brown is the only colour. The large, full-length display windows are in two planes linked by narrower, angled windows. The floor of the shop is on the same level as the pavement but separated from it by a broad band of polished stone.
The lettering of the name on the facia is executed in shiny chromium-plated steel and spotlit from the sides. The white-canvas basket blind elegantly marks the shop out from its neighbours as well as adding a well-placed note of delicacy.

| Longueur de la façade | 16 m | Fassadenlänge | 16 m | Frontage | 16 m |
| Hauteur | 4 m | Höhe | 4 m | Height | 4 m |

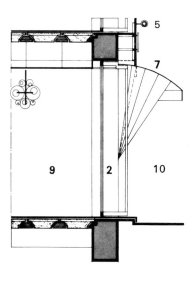

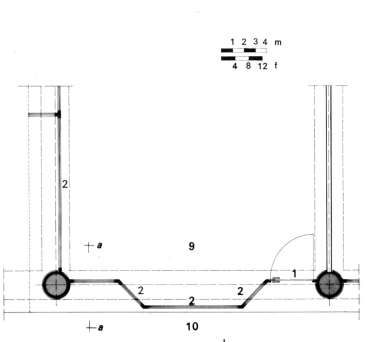

1 2 3 4 m
4 8 12 f

B

J

1. La place, l'immeuble et le magasin
2. La façade ouvrant sur la place
3. Le store-corbeille
4. Un angle et les décrochements des vitrines

1. Der Platz, das Gebäude und der Laden
2. Die zum Platz orientierte Fassade
3. Die Rollmarkise
4. Winkel und Vorsprünge der Vitrinen

1. View of the building and the shop from the square
2. The shop front facing the square
3. The basket blind
4. The angled planes of the display window

1 2

3 4

Cette pharmacie est installée à l'angle de deux voies piétonnes. La façade étroite est consacrée à l'accès de l'officine. Elle est entièrement équipée en glace. Par beau temps, les portes qui se replient mettent l'intérieur en communication directe avec la voie très passante.

La façade la plus longue présente une alternance de parties pleines et de vitrines verticales. Les premières sont réalisées en plaques d'acier spécial sur armature en menuiserie. Les huisseries des secondes sont en bois teinté. Une imposte vitrée composée de lames articulées longe cette façade en partie supérieure. Elle permet une aération bien dosée.

Le graphisme de signalisation situé dans la partie inférieure de la composition est réalisé en bois plaqué de lamifié blanc. On le retrouve sur le bandeau en béton de la maison, mais lumineux; il est en plexiglas opaque.

Diese Apotheke liegt am Schnittpunkt zweier Gehsteige. Die schmale Fassadenseite ist ganz dem Zugang zum Verkaufsraum bestimmt und besteht vollständig aus Glas. Bei schönem Wetter kann durch die aufklappbaren Türen eine unmittelbare Verbindung mit dem sehr belebten Gehsteig hergestellt werden.

Auf der längeren Fassadenseite wechseln undurchsichtige Partien und senkrechte Vitrinen miteinander ab. Erstere bestehen aus Spezialstahlplatten auf Sperrholzunterlage. Die Rahmen der Vitrinen sind aus eingefärbtem Holz. Entlang dieser Fassade verläuft ein Oberlicht, das aus verstellbaren Einzelteilen zusammengesetzt ist. Dadurch ist eine gute Regulierung der Belüftung möglich.

Die im unteren Bereich der Fassade angebrachte Beschriftung besteht aus Holz mit einem Überzug aus weißer Folie. Sie wiederholt sich auf der in Beton ausgeführten Fassadenblende des Gebäudes, allerdings in Leuchtschrift; das Material ist undurchsichtiges Plexiglas.

This chemist's shop is situated on a corner between two pedestrian streets. The narrow front is devoted to the dispensary entrance. It is entirely glazed and in fine weather the doors can be folded back to involve the interior directly in the life of the busy street.

Along the main shop front solid portions alternate with vertical windows. The former are executed in special sheet steel mounted on a wooden framework. The frames of the latter are of stained wood. A strip window comprising a number of hinged leaves runs along the top of this part of the front and provides controlled ventilation.

The lettering on the lower parts of the shop front is executed in wood covered with laminated plastic and on the concrete moulding above in translucent plexiglass lit from inside.

| | | | | |
|---|---|---|---|---|
| Longueur de la façade | 17 m | Fassadenlänge | 17 m | Frontage | 17 m |
| Hauteur | 3,20 m | Höhe | 3,20 m | Height | 3.20 m |

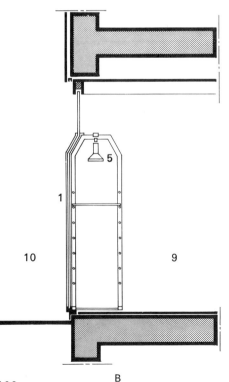

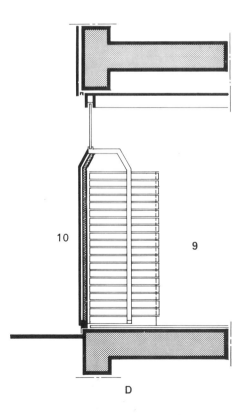

1. Les vitrines, le pilier d'angle, et à droite, le retour réservé à l'accès
2. Le pilier d'angle et l'accès sur le petit côté
3. La longue façade

1. Die Schaufenster und der Eckpfeiler, rechts die Eingangsseite
2. Der Eckpfeiler und der Eingang auf der schmalen Fassadenseite
3. Die lange Fassade

1. The display windows, showing the corner pier and, on the right, the return leading to the entrance
2. The corner pier and the entrance on the narrow front
3. The main shop front

1

2 3

# 26. Asko, München    Paul Stohrer, Arch., Stuttgart

Au centre d'un grand immeuble contemporain, une cour-patio est ouverte au public. Sur tout son pourtour, la même firme de mobilier et d'accessoires de décoration occupe les différents locaux qui sont installés en retrait d'une importante dalle en béton.
Les vitrines n'épousent pas exactement le plan général. Elles présentent une série de pans coupés de longueurs différentes. Cette particularité permet de mieux orienter les présentations vers les passants et de multiplier les effets d'ombres, de reflets et de brillances qui animent l'ensemble.
La totalité des façades est traitée d'une manière identique: soubassement métallique avec un socle en retrait, vitrine en glace claire, puis bandeau de glace émaillée bordé de deux épaisseurs inégales d'aluminium anodisé.
Le nom de la firme se répète régulièrement sur le bandeau foncé. Les lettres sont en métal laqué. Les portes sont entièrement en glace claire, les poignées en fonte d'aluminium anodisé.
L'éclairage extérieur est assuré par des lampes d'ambiance installées dans le plafond en béton, en sous-face de la dalle.

Im Zentrum eines großen, modernen Gebäudekomplexes liegt ein dem Publikum zugänglicher Innenhof. Die verschiedenen um den Hof liegenden Geschäftsräume sind hinter ein breites umlaufendes Betonband zurückgesetzt und gehören sämtlich zu der gleichen Firma für Möbel und Inneneinrichtung. Die Schaufenster weichen etwas von dem vorgegebenen Grundriß ab. Sie stellen eine Reihe gegeneinander versetzter Fassadenelemente von verschiedener Länge dar. Diese Besonderheit ermöglicht eine bessere Ausrichtung der Auslagen auf die Passanten und eine Vervielfältigung der Hell-Dunkel-Effekte, Spiegelungen und Glanzlichter, die das Ganze beleben.
Sämtliche Fassadenteile sind in der gleichen Weise ausgeführt: metallischer Unterbau mit zurückgesetztem Sockel, Vitrinen aus Schaufensterglas, darüber eine Fassadenblende aus farbigem Glas, die von zwei verschieden starken Leisten aus eloxiertem Aluminium eingefaßt ist.
Der Firmenname wiederholt sich in regelmäßigen Abständen auf der dunklen Fassadenblende. Die Buchstaben sind aus lackiertem Metall. Die Türen bestehen ganz aus Schaufensterglas, die Handgriffe aus eloxiertem Gußaluminium. Auf der Unterseite des umlaufenden Betonbandes sind Beleuchtungskörper angebracht.

In the middle of a large modern building there is a court open to the public, and all round it, set back beneath a broad concrete overhang, are a number of premises all occupied by the same furniture and decoration accessories dealer.
The display windows, rather than following the ground plan of the building, constitute a series of angled planes of varying lengths, a feature that makes it possible to beam the displays more effectively at passers-by and to increase the play of light and shade, of transparency and reflection, animating the composition as a whole.
Each front is treated in the same way and comprises a metal base with a recessed socle, a clear-glass window, and above a strip of enamelled glass bordered by two unequal widths of anodized aluminium.
The name of the firm appears at regular intervals along this dark-coloured strip in enamelled-metal lettering. The doors are entirely of clear glass and the handles of cast anodized aluminium. Outside ambient lighting is provided by lamps sunk in the underface of the concrete overhang.

| | | |
|---|---|---|
| Longueur du plus long pan coupé | 7 m | |
| Hauteur constante de la façade | 3 m | |
| Länge des längsten Fassadenelements | 7 m | |
| Konstante Höhe der Fassade | 3 m | |
| Length of longest window | 7 m | |
| Height of front (constant) | 3 m | |

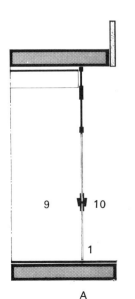

A

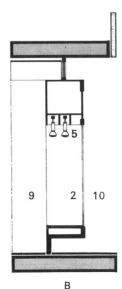

B

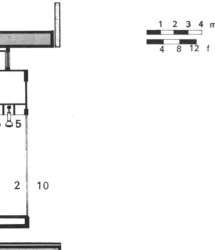

1. La cour et une série de vitrines
2. Une poignée de porte d'entrée

1. Der Innenhof und eine Gruppe von Schaufenstern
2. Handgriff einer Eingangstüre

1. The display windows along one side of the court
2. One of the door-handles

3

3. Une vitrine, et au premier plan, la sculpture située au centre de la cour
4. Une des portes d'entrée et les vitrines

3. Ein Schaufenster, im Vordergrund die in der Mitte des Hofes aufgestellte Plastik
4. Eine Eingangstüre und die Schaufenster

3. View of a display window with, in the foreground, the sculpture in the middle of the court
4. One of the doors and the display windows

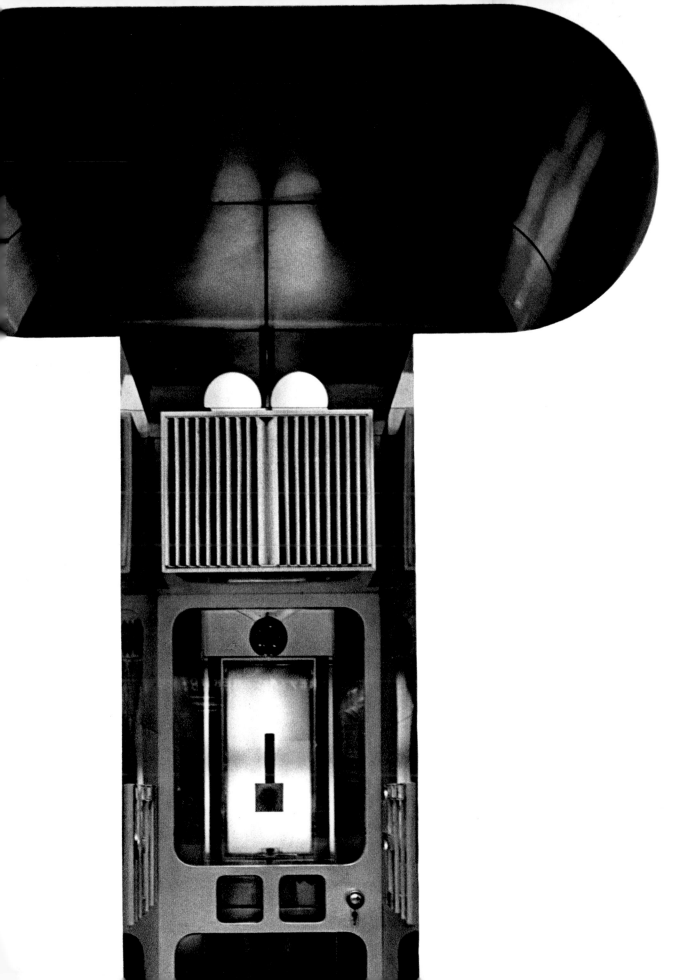

Le commerce des bougies et des objets en cire ne nécessite pas une présentation importante dans de vastes vitrines. Celles de ce magasin sont tout à fait adaptées au produit. Elles offrent en outre la particularité d'être saillantes et orientées vers le passant. La composition est en franche opposition avec la façade de l'immeuble. Seule une symétrie parfaite assure l'accord indispensable. La porte d'entrée est largement en retrait du mur extérieur. Elle est accessible par un étroit couloir (sas extérieur) surmonté d'un volume ouvert aux formes arrondies. Le fond du T ainsi créé est partiellement clos de glaces claires. L'autre matériau utilisé est l'aluminium poli traité chimiquement. Les diverses plaques sont collées ou vissées sur une structure en menuiserie.

La seule signalisation existante est le nom du fabricant réalisé en lettres d'aluminium placées de part et d'autre de l'entrée du sas, à la hauteur des vitrines.

Der Handel mit Kerzen und Wachswaren erfordert keine umfangreichen Auslagen in großen Vitrinen. Die Auslagen dieses Fachgeschäfts sind ganz auf diese Eigenschaft der Ware abgestimmt. Sie sind außerdem vorspringend angelegt und auf den Passanten hin orientiert. Die Komposition steht in klarem Gegensatz zur Gebäudefassade. Schon die vollkommene Symmetrie gewährleistet den unerläßlichen Zusammenklang. Die Eingangstüre ist weit hinter die Außenmauer zurückgesetzt. Sie wird durch einen schmalen Gang (äußere Eingangszone) erreicht, der sich nach oben in einen offenen Raum mit abgerundeten Formen erweitert. Die so geschaffene T-Form ist auf der Rückseite teilweise mit Schaufensterglas geschlossen. Als zweites Material wurde chemisch behandeltes, poliertes Aluminium verwendet. Die zahlreichen Platten sind auf eine Holzstruktur aufgeklebt oder aufgeschraubt.

Die einzige Beschilderung besteht im Namen des Fabrikanten in Aluminiumbuchstaben, die links und rechts vom äußeren Eingang und auf der Höhe der Vitrinen angebracht sind.

A shop selling candles and wax articles does not need enormous display windows and the windows of this shop are entirely suited to the product. A particular feature of them is that they project from the shop front and are turned to face the passer-by. The composition stands in unashamed contrast to the façade of the building, its perfect symmetry alone ensuring the necessary harmony. The door is set well back from the level of the front. It is reached by a narrow passage or outside vestibule, which is surmounted by a rounded open space. The resultant T-shape is partly closed off with clear glass. The other material used is polished aluminium with a chemical finish. The various sections are glued or bolted to a wooden structure.

The only graphic element is the manufacturer's name in aluminium letters on either side of the entrance passage on a level with the display windows.

| Longueur de la façade | 3,70 m | Fassadenlänge | 3,70 m | Frontage | 3.70 m |
| Hauteur | 4 m | Höhe | 4 m | Height | 4 m |

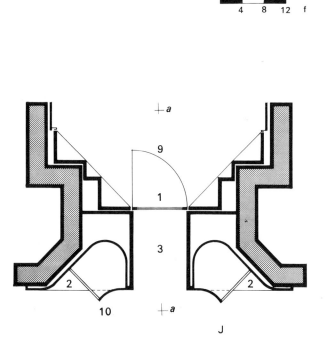

J

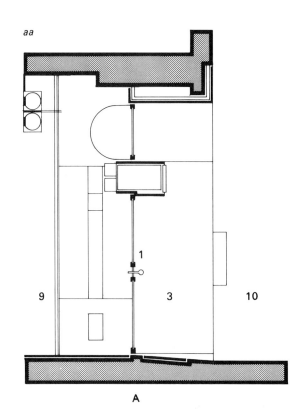

A

1. Le couloir-sas et la porte d'entrée

1. Die Eingangszone mit der Eingangstüre

1. The entrance passage and the door

1

**5**

La façade de ce magasin de mode est plaquée sur un immeuble actuel. La conception s'affirme dans la répartition des pleins et des vides étudiée avec soin afin de permettre aux passants une vision logique de l'intérieur tout en préservant une certaine intimité qui sied à ce type d'activité commerciale. La porte n'est pas vitrée de même que le centre du cercle où prennent place les volets d'aération et de climatisation. Le graphisme et la signalisation discrète sont placés à côté de la seule vitrine rectangulaire. Cette dernière et la porte assurent d'ailleurs à la composition une assise par rapport à l'horizontalité de l'architecture environnante. La totalité de la façade est réalisée en plaques d'aluminium anodisé sur structure en menuiserie.

Die Fassade dieses Modesalons ist auf ein modernes Gebäude aufgesetzt. Die Komposition zeichnet sich durch die sorgfältig ausgewogene Verteilung durchsichtiger und undurchsichtiger Flächen aus, durch die dem Passanten der nötige Einblick in das Innere gegeben, zugleich aber eine gewisse, diesem Geschäftstyp entsprechende Intimität bewahrt werden soll. Die Türe ist nicht verglast, ebensowenig die Mitte des Kreises, in der sich die Luftklappen der Belüftungs- und Klimaanlage befinden. Das Firmenzeichen und die unauffällige Beschriftung sind neben der einzigen, rechteckigen Vitrine angebracht. Diese Vitrine und die Eingangstüre geben der Komposition im übrigen ein gewisses Gegengewicht zur horizontalen Ausrichtung der umgebenden Architektur. Die Fassade insgesamt besteht aus eloxierten Aluminiumplatten auf Sperrholzunterlage.

The front of this fashion boutique is applied in a highly deliberate way to the façade of a modern building, expressing itself in a combination of solids and spaces carefully calculated to provide passers-by with a logical view of the interior while at the same time preserving the kind of intimacy appropriate to this type of trade. The door is not glazed and neither is the middle part of the circle, which houses ventilation and air-conditioning equipment. The device and the discreet lettering beneath it are fixed beside the only rectangular window. This window and the door together serve to key the composition into the horizontal context of the surrounding architecture. The entire shop front is executed in sheets of anodized aluminium mounted on a wooden structure.

| Longueur de la façade | 4,75 m |
| Hauteur | 4,75 m |

| Fassadenlänge | 4,75 m |
| Höhe | 4,75 m |

| Frontage | 4.75 m |
| Height | 4.75 m |

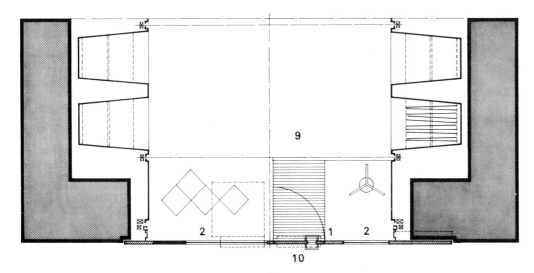

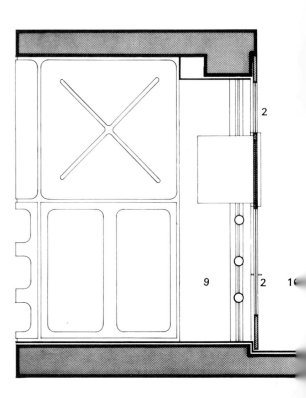

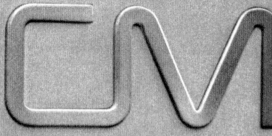

1

2

1. La vitrine rectangulaire et la porte habillée d'aluminium
2. La façade générale de l'immeuble

1. Die reckteckige Vitrine und die mit Aluminium verkleidete Eingangstüre
2. Die Gesamtfassade des Gebäudes

1. The rectangular window and the aluminium-clad door
2. The shop front in its architectural setting

3. La perspective de la façade
4. Le centre de la composition
5. La vitrine de l'intérieur; en haut à gauche, le climatiseur

3. Fluchtlinie der Geschäftsfassade
4. Das Zentrum der Komposition
5. Die Vitrinen von innen gesehen; links oben die Klimaanlage

3. View along the shop front
4. The middle portion of the composition
5. The round window seen from inside; the air-conditioner is visible top left

4

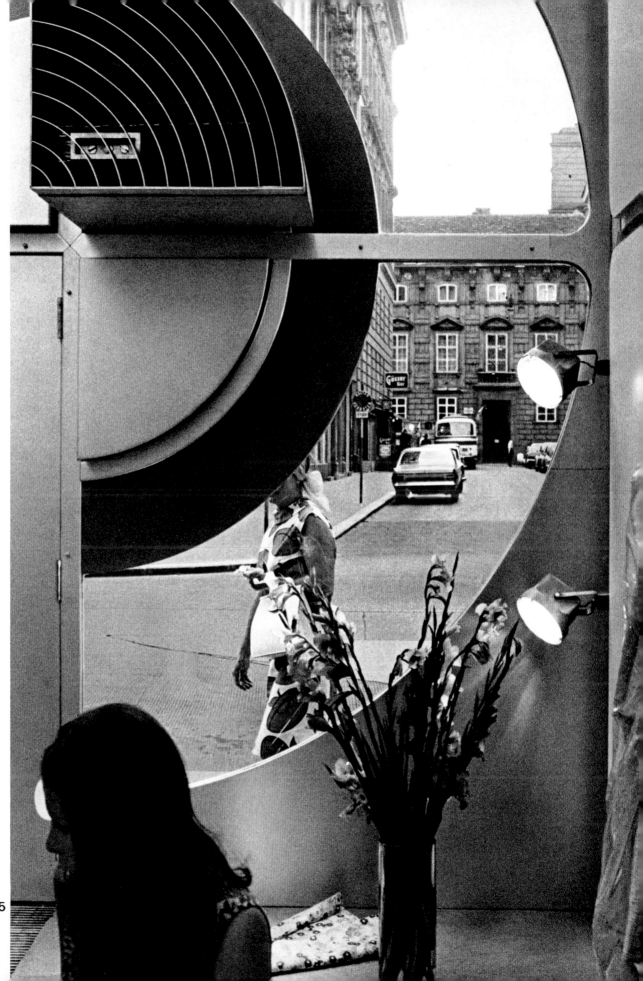

5

Suisse
Schweiz
Switzerland

Bien qu'il s'agisse d'un commerce de luxe, cette devanture a été composée dans un souci de dépouillement et de force, en harmonie avec le style du couturier très connu qui y présente ses collections «diffusion». Deux vitrines bordées d'une main courante en acier inoxydable encadrent la porte d'entrée à deux battants dont elles sont séparées par des caissons en saillie qui habillent les piliers de soutènement de l'immeuble. La totalité de ce vaste «habillage» est construit en panneaux de contre-plaqué spécial, sur une structure en bois. La finition assure l'aspect raffiné. Il s'agit d'une peinture laquée brillante dont la préparation a été particulièrement soignée.
L'enseigne en acier chromé et en plexiglas dépoli comporte un éclairage intérieur.

Obwohl es sich um ein Luxusgeschäft handelt, wurde diese Auslage bewußt nüchtern und kraftvoll gestaltet, in Übereinstimmung mit dem Stil des berühmten Modeschöpfers, der hier seine Kollektionen «diffusion» ausstellt. Zwei Vitrinen mit einer Einfassung aus nichtrostendem Stahl flankieren die zweiflügelige Eingangstüre, von der sie durch vorspringende Kästen getrennt sind, die als Verkleidung der Stützpfeiler des Gebäudes dienen. Die Gesamtheit dieser großflächigen «Verkleidung» besteht aus Spezialfurnierplatten, die auf eine Holzstruktur montiert sind. Der Anstrich bewirkt die Eleganz des Äußeren. Es handelt sich um eine Glanzlackfarbe, deren Aufbereitung besondere Sorgfalt erforderte.
Das Firmenschild aus verchromten Stahl und mattem Plexiglas ist mit einer Innenbeleuchtung ausgestattet.

Although this is a shop catering to the luxury trade its front has been designed with the same concern for simplicity and strength as characterizes the work of the well-known fashion designer who presents his 'diffusion' collections here. Two windows bordered with stainless-steel handrails flank a double-leaved door from which they are separated by projecting pilaster blocks masking the piers that support the building. The whole front is built of panels of special plywood mounted on a wooden framework. The refinement is in the finish, which employs a particularly carefully prepared high-gloss paint.
The sign, of chromium-plated steel and frosted plexiglass, is lit from inside.

| | |
|---|---|
| Longueur de la façade | 9,60 m |
| Hauteur | 3,70 m |

| | |
|---|---|
| Fassadenlänge | 9,60 m |
| Höhe | 3,70 m |

| | |
|---|---|
| Frontage | 9.60 m |
| Height | 3.70 m |

1.  La façade dans sa totalité
2.  Les poignées des portes d'entrée
3.  Une vitrine

1.  Die gesamte Fassade
2.  Die Handgriffe der Eingangstüre
3.  Eine Vitrine

1.  View of the whole shop front
2.  The door-handles
3.  One of the display windows

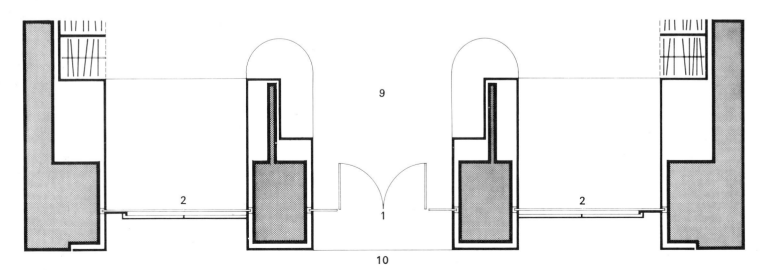

J

**1**

**2**

**3**

Ce magasin de mobilier contemporain est installé sur deux niveaux, à la base d'une vaste et belle maison ancienne restaurée avec soin.

Pour faire pénétrer la lumière naturelle au cœur du sous-sol (niveau inférieur), l'architecte a ouvert dans la cour intérieure de la maison — qui est de plus un passage pour piétons —, un patio en creux. Le centre de ce patio est réalisé en galets dans un lit de mortier. Une jardinière en béton garnie de végétation ceinture l'ouverture de plan carré.

Le sous-œuvre a été repris en béton. Ainsi les bandeaux surplombant les vitrines, leurs soubassements et les piliers de soutènement ont été conservés brut de décoffrage. Il en est de même de l'escalier aux formes courbes qui fait communiquer le patio et les portes d'entrée avec la cour supérieure. Les glaces claires des vitrines sont montées dans de fins profils en aluminium. Les poignées des portes en glace claire sont en aluminium anodisé et verni.

La nuit venue, le patio est éclairé par des spots installés à l'intérieur du magasin. Les lettres de la raison sociale en tôle laquée comportent un éclairage intérieur qui les détache du bandeau.

Dieses Fachgeschäft für moderne Einrichtungen liegt auf zwei Ebenen im unteren Geschoß eines großen und schönen alten Hauses, das sorgfältig renoviert worden ist.

Um das Tageslicht bis in das Innere des Tiefgeschosses (untere Ebene) eindringen zu lassen, wurde vom Architekten im Innenhof des Gebäudes (der zugleich als Fußgängerpassage dient) ein Patio ausgeschachtet. Das Zentrum dieses Patio ist mit Flußkieseln in einem Mörtelbett ausgelegt. Das Fundament ist in Beton ausgeführt. Die Blenden über den Vitrinen, deren Unterbau, sowie die Stützpfeiler wurden in Schalbeton belassen. Die gleiche Ausführung zeigt die geschwungene Treppe, die den Patio und die Eingangstüren mit dem oberen Hof verbindet. Die Scheiben der Vitrinen werden von dünnen Profilleisten aus Aluminium festgehalten. Die Handgriffe der Glastüren bestehen aus eloxiertem Aluminium mit einem Firnißüberzug. Rings um die Öffnung des ausgeschachteten Quadrats läuft eine bepflanzte Betonwanne.

Nachts wird der Patio von Spots angestrahlt, die im Inneren des Geschäfts montiert sind. Die aus lakkiertem Blech bestehenden Buchstaben des Firmenschilds sind mit einer Innenbeleuchtung ausgestattet, durch die sie von der dahinterliegenden Blende abgehoben sind.

This modern-furniture shop occupies premises on two levels at the bottom of a large and very fine old house that has been carefully restored.

In order to daylight the basement (the lower of the two levels) the architect has dug out a patio in the internal courtyard of the house, which is also a pedestrian passage. The middle of this patio is floored with cobbles bedded in mortar. The foundations have been recast in concrete, and on the lintels above the display windows, on the sills below, and on the supporting members the shuttering marks have been left exposed. The curving flight of steps linking the patio and entrance with the courtyard above is likewise unrendered. The clear-glass display windows are mounted in thin aluminium frames. The doors are of clear glass and the handles of varnished anodized aluminium. A plant trough filled with vegetation runs round the top of the square opening.

At night the patio is spotlit from inside the shop. The lettering of the name is done in enamelled sheet metal with lighting inside to make it stand out from the concrete behind it.

| Dimensions du patio | 6,80 × 6,80 m | Ausmaße des Patio | 6,80 × 6,80 m | Dimensions of patio | 6.80 × 6.80 m |
| Hauteur | 3,40 m | Höhe | 3,40 m | Height | 3.40 m |

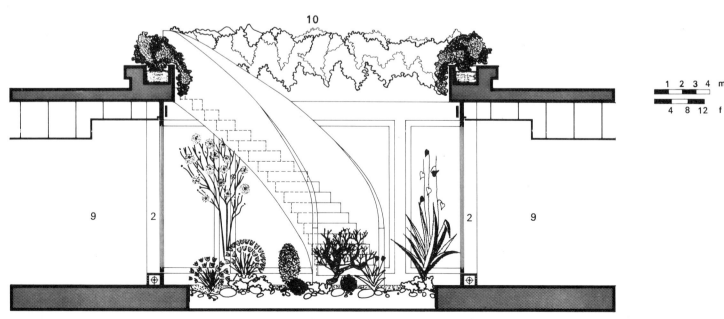

1

2

3

1. Départ de l'escalier vers le patio
2. Les vitrines et l'escalier
3. Le bandeau des vitrines et la jardinière supérieure

1. Treppe zum Patio hinunter
2. Die Vitrinen und die Treppe
3. Die Blende über den Vitrinen und der Pflanztrog

1. The top of the flight of steps leading down to the patio
2. The display windows and part of the steps
3. The facia and the plant trough above the display windows

Le rez-de-chaussée et le sous-sol de cet immeuble sont occupés par plusieurs magasins ouvrant sur une galerie fermée. La vitrine d'horlogerie-bijouterie prenant jour sur la rue est le prolongement d'un de ces magasins. La façade inférieure de la construction comporte donc cette vitrine surmontée d'une surface vitrée éclairant un niveau intermédiaire, le hall précédant les portes d'entrée à la galerie et l'accès au couloir de l'immeuble.
Les piliers et les angles des parties pleines de l'armature métallique sont arrondis. L'habillage, comme celui de la façade, est réalisé en tôle d'acier laqué mat. Pour subdiviser horizontalement la composition, une structure assez plate est fixée en avancée de la façade extérieure, à environ trois mètres du sol. Un retour perpendiculaire a permis de peindre les lettres composant le nom de la firme présente la plus importante.
Le sol de la galerie et des magasins est au niveau du trottoir extérieur. Celui du hall est tendu d'un revêtement de caoutchouc.

Im Erd- und Tiefgeschoß dieses Gebäudes liegen mehrere Geschäfte, die von einer geschlossenen Galerie aus zugänglich sind. Die der Straße zugewandte Vitrine des Uhren- und Juweliergeschäfts stellt die Verlängerung eines dieser Geschäftsräume dar. Der untere Fassadenbereich des Gebäudes enthält diese Vitrine mit einer darüberliegenden Verglasung, durch die das Licht auf ein Zwischengeschoß fällt, außerdem die den Türen zur Galerie vorgelagerte Halle und den Zugang zum Flur des Gebäudes.
Die Stützpfeiler sowie die Ecken in der Metallverkleidung sind abgerundet. Die Verkleidung besteht wie bei der Gebäudefassade aus mattlackiertem Stahlblech. Um eine waagerechte Untergliederung der Komposition zu erreichen, wurde eine relativ flache Platte in etwa drei Meter Höhe über dem Boden vor die Außenfassade gesetzt. Auf eine rechtwinklig dazu liegende Blende wurde der Name der hier vorgestellten, bedeutendsten Firma aufgemalt.
Der Boden der Galerie und der Geschäftsräume liegt auf der Höhe des äußeren Fußgängerbereichs. Der Fußboden der Halle ist mit einem Gummibelag ausgestattet.

Ground floor and basement of this building are occupied by a number of shops that open into an inside gallery. This watchmaker's and jeweller's display window giving onto the street is an extension of one of those shops. The lower part of the façade of the building thus comprises this display window with a glazed area above it lighting an intermediate level, the hallway leading to the gallery entrance, and the entrance to the corridor of the building.
The pillars and the angles of the solid portions of the metal armature are rounded. Like the rest of the façade they are clad in matt-enamelled sheet steel. A flattish structure mounted some three metres from the ground and projecting from the façade has the effect of subdividing the composition horizontally. Painted in large letters on a vertical extension of this is the name of the firm.
The floors of gallery and shops are on the same level as the pavement. The hallway is floored with rubber matting.

| | | | | | | |
|---|---|---|---|---|---|---|
| Longueur de la façade | 18,30 m | Fassadenlänge | 18,30 m | Frontage | 18.30 m |
| Hauteur | 4,65 m | Höhe | 4,65 m | Height | 4.65 m |

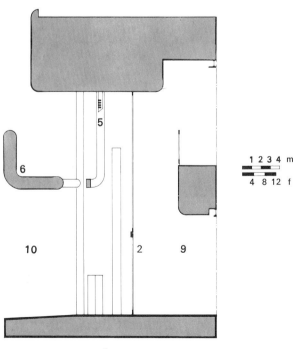

B

**1**

1. La façade inférieure
2. La façade générale
3. L'angle d'un des piliers et le revêtement du sol du hall
4. Le bandeau en tôle laquée

1. Der untere Fassadenbereich
2. Die Gebäudefassade
3. Detail eines der Stützpfeiler und der Bodenbelag der Halle
4. Die Blende aus lackiertem Metall

1. The lower part of the façade
2. General view of the façade
3. Detail of the bottom of a pillar, showing the rubber matting
4. The enamelled sheet steel structure bearing the sign

**2**

**3**

**4**

Italie
Italien
Italy

Cette galerie de meubles, de luminaires et d'objets contemporains s'étant installée dans une maison ancienne, il était impossible de concevoir une façade rajoutée. Aussi, pour clore la vaste arcade en plein cintre et les deux fenêtres latérales, le choix s'est porté sur la glace claire qui assure une grande luminosité au local et transforme les ouvertures d'origine en vitrines actuelles. Les huisseries sont en métal laqué. La porte est bien intégrée à l'architecture: elle est inscrite dans une épaisse huisserie en métal également laqué, dont la partie supérieure est demi-circulaire. Le montage de la porte est réalisé sur pivots. La poignée constituée d'un tube chromé confirme l'esprit général que l'on retrouve aussi dans le cercle peint sur la glace où sont juxtaposées les lettres composant le nom de la galerie.

Diese Galerie für Möbel, Beleuchtungskörper und moderne Einrichtungsgegenstände wurde in einem alten Haus untergebracht, das eine völlig neue Fassadengestaltung nicht zuließ. Man entschied sich daher dafür, den großen Arkadenbogen und die beiden seitlichen Fensteröffnungen mit durchsichtigem Schaufensterglas abzuschließen, wodurch der Ladenraum viel Licht erhält und die ursprünglichen Maueröffnungen in moderne Auslagen verwandelt werden. Die Rahmen bestehen aus lackiertem Metall. Auch die Eingangstüre ist gut in die Architektur integriert: Sie ist in einen ebenfalls lackierten, breiten Metallrahmen eingehängt, der im oberen Teil halbkreisförmig gebogen ist. Die Türe ist auf Scharnieren montiert. Der aus einer Chromstange bestehende Türgriff verdeutlicht den Geist dieser Konzeption ebenso wie der auf das Schaufensterglas aufgemalte Kreis, in den der Name der Galerie eingesetzt ist.

The architecture of the old house occupied by this furniture and furnishing accessories gallery ruled out the addition of a shop front proper.
The solution adopted for the enormous semicircular arch and the two flanking windows was to fill them with clear glass, thus flooding the interior with light and turning the original apertures into highly original display windows. The frames are of enamelled metal. The door, mounted on pivots inside a broad enamelled-metal frame with a semicircular top, constitutes a visual echo of the aperture it occupies. The chromium-plated tubular handle confirms the general tone, as does the lettering of the name of the firm painted inside a circle on the glass above the door.

| | | | |
|---|---|---|---|
| Longueur de la façade | 7 m | Fassadenlänge | 7 m | Frontage | 7 m |
| Hauteur | 3,80 m | Höhe | 3,80 m | Height | 3.80 m |

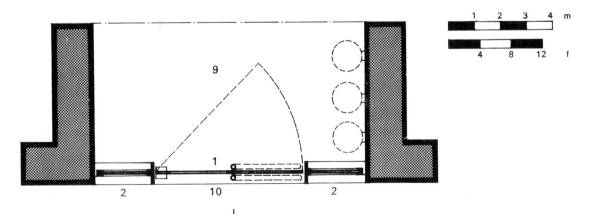

1. La façade de la maison et les trois ouvertures

1. Die Gebäudefassade und die drei Maueröffnungen

1. The façade with its three apertures

2. La porte d'entrée
3. L'ouverture centrale vue de l'intérieur
4. Le pivot supérieur de la porte

2. Die Eingangstüre
3. Die zentrale Maueröffnungung von innen gesehen
4. Das obere Scharnier der Eingangstüre

2. The door
3. The middle aperture from inside
4. The top door pivot

Dans le quartier très touristique et «à la mode» où se trouve cette petite boutique d'objets décoratifs, les maisons sont anciennes, les tonalités de leur crépi délicates et ensoleillées. Pour singulariser la composition de cette devanture tout en l'harmonisant à la maison, l'architecte a choisi pour la vitrine et la porte en glace claire un encadrement saillant en acier chromé et en glace émaillée. Dans les parties verticales de cet encadrement se loge une grille de protection articulée qui est laquée en bleu. De jour, elle est dissimulée par des volets pris dans le retour de l'encadrement.
La seule signalisation est située sur la porte. Les petites lettres sont en acier chromé comme la poignée.

| | |
|---|---|
| Longueur de la façade | 2,20 m |
| Hauteur | 2,60 m |

Die Häuser des viel besuchten Touristenviertels, in dem sich diese kleine Boutique für Dekorationsgegenstände befindet, sind alt, ihr Verputz zeigt sanfte, sonnenverbrannte Töne. Um die Komposition charakteristisch zu gestalten und gleichzeitig harmonisch in das Haus einzufügen, wurde vom Architekten vor die Vitrine und die durchsichtige Glastüre ein Rahmen aus verchromtem Stahl und farbigem Glas gesetzt. In den senkrechten Teilen

dieses Rahmens befindet sich ein aus mehreren Gliedern bestehendes, blau lackiertes Schutzgitter. Tagsüber ist das Gitter hinter Blenden verborgen, die an der Eckseite des Rahmens befestigt sind.
Das einzige vorhandene Firmenschild ist über der Türe angebracht. Die kleinformatigen Buchstaben bestehen wie der Türgriff aus verchromten Stahl.

| | |
|---|---|
| Fassadenlänge | 2,20 m |
| Höhe | 2,60 m |

The fashionable and tourist-frequented quarter in which this boutique selling decorative articles is situated consists of old houses with façades of sun-baked plaster in a variety of delicate hues. To give his composition distinction and yet keep it in harmony with the building the architect chose to enclose the display window and the glass door within a projecting frame of chromium-plated steel and enamelled glass. The uprights of the frame house a hinged security grille, painted blue. By day this is concealed by means of shutters on the return faces.
The only sign is on the door, in small letters executed like the handle in chromium-plated steel.

| | |
|---|---|
| Frontage | 2.20 m |
| Height | 2.60 m |

1. La grille de protection semi-dépliée
2. Le volet latéral fermé
3. La façade ceinturée d'acier chromé

1. Das halb ausgeklappte Schutzgitter
2. Die seitlich angebrachte Blende in geschlossenem Zustand
3. Die Fassade mit ihrer Chromeinfassung

1. The security grille partially unfolded
2. The shutter in the closed position
3. The shop front is framed in chromium-plated steel

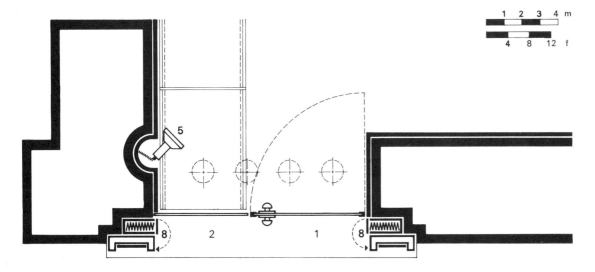

J

Ce magasin occupe un volume assez profond à la base d'un immeuble actuel sans caractère très affirmé. Il est destiné à la présentation d'un revêtement de papier laqué, et tient aussi lieu de galerie d'art contemporain.
La façade présente deux grands pans inclinés: celui des glaces de la vitrine et de la porte, et dans une pente inversée, celui du bandeau supérieur. La construction est réalisée en bois massif pour les huisseries et les montants, et en contre-plaqué traité spécialement pour un usage extérieur sur armature en menuiserie pour les surfaces pleines. Le tout est laqué avec soin dans la même peinture blanche, avec une finition satinée. La poignée de la porte est un tube de section ronde barrant la glace dedans comme dehors. Le seuil de la vitrine et la marche d'entrée sont en pierre polie, ainsi que le parement des piliers latéraux et de leurs retours intérieurs.
Les lettres de la raison sociale, au volume très puissant, sont réalisées en tôle d'acier laqué avec une face en plexiglas; elles comportent un éclairage intérieur.

Dieses Geschäft nimmt einen ziemlich tiefen Raum im Erdgeschoß eines modernen Gebäudes ein, das keinen besonders ausgeprägten Charakter besitzt. Es dient als Ausstellungsraum für eine bestimmte Wandverkleidung aus Lackpapier und ist zugleich eine Galerie für zeitgenössische Kunst.
Die Fassade zeigt zwei große, gegeneinander geneigte Elemente: die Glasfläche der Vitrine und der Eingangstüre und die Fassadenblende. Die Rahmen und Stützen der Konstruktion bestehen aus massivem Holz, die Füllflächen sind in Schiffsfurnier auf Holz montiert. Das Ganze erhielt einen seidenmatten Lackanstrich in weißer Farbe. Der Türgriff hat die Form einer Röhre mit rundem Profil und verläuft auf der Innen- und Außenseite quer zur Glasscheibe. Das Sims der Vitrine und die Stufe am Eingang sind wie die Verkleidung der Seitenpfeiler und ihrer Innenflächen aus poliertem Stein.
Die auffallend großen Buchstaben des Firmennamens aus lackiertem Stahlblech mit einer Vorderseite aus Plexiglas sind mit einer Innenbeleuchtung ausgestattet.

This shop occupies premises running back some way into the ground floor of a rather characterless modern building. It combines the functions of wallpaper showroom and gallery of contemporary art.
The front is distinguished by two large inclined surfaces, namely the panes of the display window and the door and, in the opposite plane, the facia above. It is constructed of timber for the frames and uprights and plywood mounted on a wooden framework for the solid portions. The whole front is carefully painted with a satin-finish white paint. The door-handle, inside and out, consists of a cylindrical bar across the glazed portion. The step running along the whole front is of polished stone, as is the cladding of the lateral pillars and their returns.
The enormous lettering is executed in enamelled sheet steel, fronted with plexiglass and lit from inside.

| | | | |
|---|---|---|---|
| Longueur de la façade | 4 m | Fassadenlänge | 4 m |
| Hauteur | 3,30 m | Höhe | 3,30 m |

| | |
|---|---|
| Frontage | 4 m |
| Height | 3.30 m |

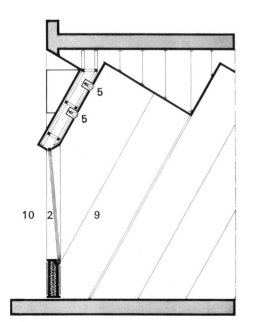

B

1

2

1.  Perspective de la façade; les pans coupés sont très marqués
2.  La façade en vue frontale

1.  Fluchtlinie der Fassade; die schrägen Fassadenelemente treten deutlich hervor
2.  Frontalansicht der Fassade

1.  View along the shop front, showing the distinctive inclined planes
2.  View of the whole shop front

3.  La vitrine et la porte d'entrée fermée
4.  La porte entrouverte

3.  Die Vitrine und die geschlossene Eingangstüre
4.  Halboffene Eingangstüre

3.  The display window, showing the door in the closed position
4.  The door ajar

3

4

Aménagé au rez-de-chaussée d'un très beau et ancien palais, ce magasin de couture n'offre au passant aucune vitrine de présentation. Sa renommée le lui permet.

Les vastes ouvertures rectangulaires cernées d'un cadre de pierre mouluré font chacune l'objet de compositions particulières mais très apparentées par le rythme des obliques. Le matériau utilisé est la tôle d'acier laqué. Les portes d'entrée en retrait de la façade forment des petits sas extérieurs. Ces portes sont en glace claire comme le fond des fentes étroites et les triangles supérieurs qui assurent l'éclairement de la mezzanine du magasin. La ventilation de ce niveau s'effectue grâce à de petits cylindres se projetant en légère saillie au centre des bandes claires qui animent la composition extérieure.

La seule signalisation est située dans les fentes obliques prenant naissance dans le sas d'entrée. Ce sont des lettres découpées à l'extrémité des cylindres métalliques comportant un éclairage intérieur.

Dieser Modesalon im Erdgeschoß eines schönen alten Palazzo zeigt dem Passanten keine einzige Auslage. Aufgrund seiner Berühmtheit kann er darauf verzichten.

Die großflächigen, von einem profilierten Steinrahmen eingefaßten, rechteckigen Maueröffnungen sind sämtlich auf individuelle, durch den Rhythmus der schrägen Linien jedoch einander ähnliche Weise gestaltet. Das verwendete Material ist lackiertes Stahlblech. Die etwas hinter die Fassadenmauer zurückgesetzten Eingangstüren lassen kleine Außenzonen frei. Diese Türen bestehen aus Glas, ebenso die Füllung der schmalen Schlitze und die oben eingesetzten Dreiecke, durch die Licht auf das Zwischengeschoß im Inneren fällt. Die Belüftung dieses Geschosses erfolgt durch kleine Zylinder in der Mitte der hellen schrägen Bänder, die die Außengestaltung beleben.

Die einzige vorhandene Beschriftung befindet sich in den schrägverlaufenden Spalten der Eingangszone. Die Buchstaben sind auf Metallzylinder gesetzt, die mit einer Innenbeleuchtung ausgestattet sind.

This fashion shop, which occupies premises on the ground floor of a very fine old palace, is so well-known that it can afford to dispense with display windows.

Each of the enormous rectangular apertures framed with stone mouldings forms an individual composition, though the three are closely related by their use of oblique elements. The material employed is enamelled sheet steel. The doors, which are set back from the façade, leaving small outside vestibules, are of clear glass, as are the backs of the narrow slits and the triangles above that light the mezzanine. Ventilation of the mezzanine is by small cylinders that project slightly from the middle of the oblique strips characterizing the frontal view.

The only sign is in the oblique slits starting from the entrance vestibule. The letters are cut out of the ends of metal cylinders with lights inside.

| | | | | | |
|---|---|---|---|---|---|
| Largeur de chaque ouverture d'origine | 2,20 m | Breite der ursprünglichen Maueröffnungen | 2,20 m | Width of original apertures | 2.20 m |
| Hauteur | 7,30 m | Höhe | 7,30 m | Height | 7.30 m |

M

1. L'immeuble à l'angle de deux rues
2. La façade et ses deux portes d'entrée

1. Das an einer Straßenecke gelegene Gebäude
2. Die Fassade mit den zwei Eingangstüren

1. The shop occupies a corner site
2. The shop front, showing the two doors

3

5

4

Cet institut de beauté et de soins est installé au premier étage d'une vieille maison, dans une petite rue pittoresque. Le rez-de-chaussée ne comprend qu'un mini-vestibule d'où part un escalier. La façade est réduite mais déborde de la porte d'entrée sur l'un des côtés. Cet élargissement a permis de créer une petite vitrine. La construction est réalisée en aluminium anodisé de deux tons, sur une armature métallique. Un bandeau en avancée sur la façade, de la même largeur que les trois verticales, structure la composition. Des spots y sont encastrés. Durant les heures d'inactivité, une porte en acier poli assure la fermeture. Un jeu de barreaux verticaux et horizontaux subdivise cette porte en rectangles équipés chacun d'une glace teintée.
Un caisson surplombe la porte; il renferme de la lumière qui éclaire au travers d'un plexiglas coloré les lettres découpées. Le même principe est utilisé au-dessus de la vitrine pour signaler le nom de l'esthéticienne.

Dieses Kosmetikinstitut befindet sich im ersten Stock eines alten, in einer malerischen Gasse gelegenen Hauses. Das Erdgeschoß besteht lediglich aus einer kleinen Halle, von der aus eine Treppe nach oben führt. Die Fassade ist schmal, führt jedoch auf einer Seite über die Eingangstüre hinaus. Diese Erweiterung ermöglichte den Einbau einer kleinen Vitrine. Die Konstruktion besteht aus zweifarbig eloxiertem Aluminium auf einer Metallunterkonstruktion. Eine aufgesetzte Blende von derselben Breite wie die drei vertikalen Elemente gliedert die Fassade. Sie ist mit eingebauten Spots bestückt. Wenn das Institut geschlossen ist, sichert eine Türe aus poliertem Stahl das Haus. Waagerechte und senkrechte Stäbe unterteilen die Türe in Rechtecke, von denen in jedes eine farbige Glasscheibe eingesetzt ist.
Die Kassette über der Türe besteht aus farbigem Plexiglas und besitzt eine Innenbeleuchtung, vor der sich die aufgesetzten Buchstaben abzeichnen. Dasselbe Prinzip wurde bei der über der Vitrine angebrachten Beschilderung angewandt.

This beauty parlour occupies premises on the first floor of an old house in a charming little street. The ground floor consists of no more than a tiny vestibule from which a staircase leads up to the parlour itself, and the shop front merely comprises the door and a small extension to one side. The extension accommodates a small display window. The structure is executed in anodized aluminium in two tones, mounted on a metal framework. A projecting facia of the same width as the uprights and housing three spots adds interest to the composition. When the business is closed a polished-metal door seals the premises. Mullions and transoms divide this door into a series of rectangles, each of which is filled with a pane of tinted glass.
A box above the door houses a lamp illuminating the lettering cut in its coloured-plexiglass front. The same principle is used for the beautician's name above the display window.

| | | | | | |
|---|---|---|---|---|---|
| Longueur de la façade | 1,80 m | Fassadenlänge | 1,80 m | Frontage | 1.80 m |
| Hauteur | 2,60 m | Höhe | 2,60 m | Height | 2.60 m |

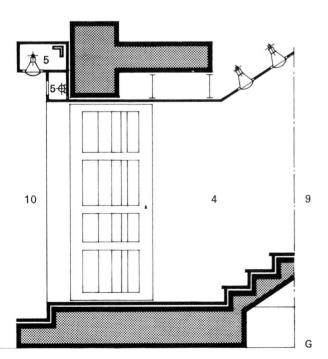

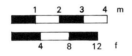

1.  La porte
2.  La façade inscrite dans la vieille maison

1.  Die Eingangstüre
2.  Die in das Haus eingegliederte Geschäftsfassade

1.  The door
2.  The shop front in its ancient setting

1                                                                2

Espagne
Spanien
Spain

Cette maison de couture bénéficie d'une assez large ouverture sur la rue et d'une importante surface intérieure. Ceci a permis de réserver, à côté de la grande vitrine circulaire, un vaste hall d'accès situé en contrebas et accessible par plusieurs marches. Ce hall précède l'entrée proprement dite formée de deux portes en glace claire au centre d'un cercle presque complet, surmonté d'un évidement de forme identique, également équipé d'une glace claire.

Le hall orné de plantes vertes est clos durant les heures et jours de fermeture par deux portes-volets, en tôle laquée blanc. Les deux initiales du couturier y ont été formées en creux. Le matériau de finition du hall, de la façade et de la vitrine est du plâtre sur un fond en maçonnerie traditionnelle. L'application de la peinture laquée a fait l'objet d'un soin tout particulier, assurant à l'ensemble une qualité parfaitement en accord avec l'activité commerciale et le quartier résidentiel.

Le hall est éclairé par des spots dissimulés dans la verdure. Il n'existe ni éclairage extérieur, ni signalisation spéciale.

Dieses Modehaus weist eine ziemlich breite Öffnung zur Straßenseite und eine große Innenfläche auf. Dadurch blieb neben der großen, kreisförmigen Vitrine Platz für eine großzügige Eingangshalle, die etwas tiefer gelegen und über mehrere Stufen zu erreichen ist. Diese Halle ist dem eigentlichen Eingang vorgelagert, der aus zwei durchsichtigen Glastüren besteht, die in eine fast vollständig kreisförmige Öffnung eingehängt sind; darüber befindet sich eine zweite, identisch geformte und ebenfalls durchsichtig verglaste Maueröffnung.

Außerhalb der Verkaufszeiten wird die mit Grünpflanzen dekorierte Halle durch zwei Türläden aus weißlackiertem Blech abgeschlossen, in die die beiden Initialen des Modeschöpfers eingestanzt sind. Das Verputzmaterial der Halle und der Schaufensterfassade besteht aus Gips auf konventionell gemauertem Untergrund. Der Lackanstrich verleiht dem Ganzen eine besondere Note, die dem Typus des Geschäfts und der Eleganz des Viertels entspricht.

Die Halle wird von Spots beleuchtet, die in den Grünpflanzen verborgen sind. Auf eine Außenbeleuchtung sowie auf ein eigenes Firmenschild wurde verzichtet.

The fact that this fashion house has a broad street frontage and is generously provided with floor space made it possible to accommodate, beside the large, round window, a sunken vestibule reached by a short flight of steps. This vestibule precedes the entrance proper—a double glass door situated in the centre of an almost complete circle and surmounted by a further circle, both circles being filled with clear glass.

The vestibule with its decorative plants is closed off when the shop is closed by means of two white-enamelled sheet steel security doors in which the fashion designer's initials are recessed. The vestibule and the display window surround are finished with plaster applied to traditional masonry. The whole has been gloss-painted with particular care in order to make it harmonize both with the nature of the business conducted here and with the residential quarter in which the shop is situated.

The vestibule is lit by spots concealed in the foliage. There is no outside lighting and no sign.

| | | | |
|---|---|---|---|
| Longueur de la façade | 11 m | Fassadenlänge | 11 m | Frontage | 11 m |
| Hauteur | 5 m | Höhe | 5 m | Height | 5 m |
| Profondeur du hall | 4,60 m | Tiefe der Halle | 4,60 m | Depth of vestibule | 4.60 m |

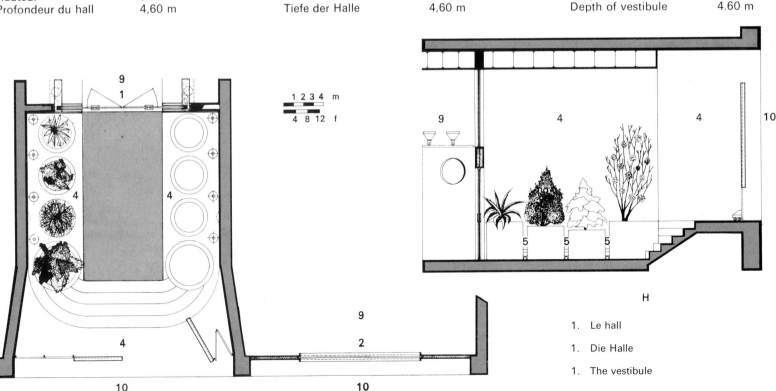

1. Le hall

1. Die Halle

1. The vestibule

2. Les deux portes de protection fermées
3. 4. Détail des lettres en creux dans les portes-volets de fermeture
5. Support roulant des portes-volets

2. Die Schutztüre in geschlossenem Zustand
3. 4. Detail der in die Türläden eingestanzten Buchstaben
5. Auf Rollen laufendes Stützlager der Türläden

2. The security doors in the closed position
3. 4. Detail of the recessed lettering in the security doors
5. The sliding support of the security doors

6. La façade un jour de fermeture
7. Les portes d'entrée
8. Le hall vu de l'intérieur du magasin

6. Ansicht der Fassade außerhalb der Verkaufszeiten
7. Die Eingangstüren
8. Die Halle von innen her gesehen

6. View of the whole front shop with the security doors closed
7. The entrance doors
8. The vestibule from inside the shop

8

## 38.  Valcarcel, Madrid    Antonio Bonamusa, Arch., Barcelona

Destiné à la présentation de carrelages et de produits céramiques, ce magasin offre une façade extrêmement sobre et lumineuse. Une vitrine étroite succède à une vitrine plus haute, jouxtant la porte d'entrée. La bande horizontale est équilibrée par la verticalité de quatre cylindres en métal chromé entourant cette porte, et par le décrochement au fond duquel s'élève, derrière l'habillage général, un des deux piliers de soutènement de l'immeuble. L'autre pilier se trouve à la jonction des deux vitrines; il est plaqué de miroir. La poignée-boule de la porte et les profilés cernant les surfaces planes sont également en métal chromé. La marche d'entrée formant le seuil est en acier inoxydable. Le matériau des plaques de parement est un aggloméré de poudre de marbre blanc avec un poli miroir.
Les lettres de la raison sociale sont en tôle laquée avec un équipement intérieur en tube néon.

Dieser für die Ausstellung von Fliesen und Keramik bestimmte Geschäftsraum zeigt eine äußerst nüchterne, helle Fassade. An ein schmales Schaufenster schließt ein höheres an, das neben der Eingangstüre liegt. Das waagerechte Band findet ein Gegengewicht in der senkrechten Anordnung von vier verchromten Metallzylindern seitlich der Türe und in der Mauervertiefung, bewirkt durch einen der beiden Stützpfeiler des Gebäudes, der von der Fassadenverkleidung verdeckt ist. Der zweite Pfeiler befindet sich zwischen beiden Schaufenstern und ist verspiegelt. Der Türgriff und die einfassenden Profile bestehen ebenfalls aus verchromtem Metall. Die Türschwelle besteht aus nichtrostendem Stahl. Die Verkleidung bilden Werksteinplatten aus pulverisiertem weißem Marmor mit Glanzschliff.
Die Buchstaben des Firmennamens aus lackiertem Blech sind mit einer Neonbeleuchtung ausgestattet.

This tile and ceramic-products showroom presents an extremely sober and luminous front. A narrow display window leads into a deeper display window abutting against the door. This horizontal band is balanced by four upright cylinders of chromium-plated metal flanking the door and by a recess above two of the cylinders exposing one of the building's two supporting pillars. The other pillar occurs at the junction of the two display windows and is faced with mirror. The spherical door-handle and the sectional members enclosing the flat surfaces are also of chromium-plated metal. The doorstep is stainless steel. The cladding sheets are made of powdered white marble agglomerate with a mirror finish.
The name of the shop appears in enamelled sheet metal letters with neon tubing inside.

| | | | | |
|---|---|---|---|---|
| Longueur de la façade | 8 m | Fassadenlänge | 8 m | Frontage | 8 m |
| Hauteur | 4,20 m | Höhe | 4,20 m | Height | 4.20 m |

1. La façade et ses deux modules de vitrine
2. Une perspective de l'ensemble

1. Die Fassade mit ihren zwei Schaufenstern
2. Fluchtlinie der Fassade

1. General view of the shop front, showing the two display windows
2. Looking along the front

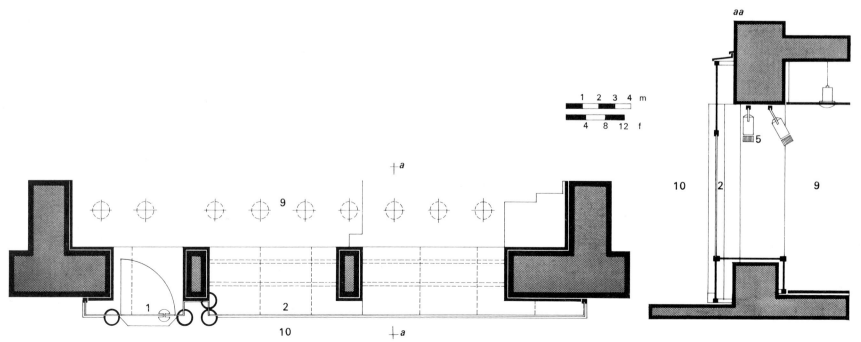

150

1

2

3. Deux des cylindres autour du décrochement en creux
4. L'angle des deux vitrines
5. La base d'un cylindre et le seuil de la porte
6. La porte d'entrée et une vitrine

3. Zwei der vertikalen Zylinder
4. Die gemeinsame Ecke der beiden Vitrinen
5. Der untere Teil eines Zylinders und die Türschwelle
6. Die Eingangstüre und ein Schaufenster

3. The two metal cylinders flanking the pillar recess
4. Detail of the corner between the two windows
5. The bottom of one of the metal cylinders, showing part of the doorstep
6. The door and one of the display windows

Voici un petit salon de coiffure dont la façade, traitée avec beaucoup de fantaisie, est en parfaite harmonie avec l'architecture contemporaine de l'immeuble qui l'accueille.
Les huisseries sont en aluminium. Les impostes se trouvent au niveau général du mur de la maison, la partie inférieure en légère avancée. Les glaces ont reçu une argenture très élaborée selon une tendance propre à l'art optique. Les zones non argentées sont restées en glace claire et laissent filtrer la lumière et les regards. Seule la porte est totalement translucide; sa poignée est une plaque de glace très épaisse. Cette porte est surmontée d'une structure réalisée en plexiglas sur laquelle la raison sociale et un graphisme sont laqués. Le soir venu, deux spots puissants éclairent la structure, et, par reflets, font miroiter comme les lumières de la rue les centaines de petits miroirs de la composition.

Longueur de la façade     2,65 m
Hauteur                   2,70 m

Die Fassade dieses kleinen Frisiersalons ist mit viel Phantasie und in vollkommener Harmonie mit der modernen Architektur des Hauses gestaltet, in dem er untergebracht ist.
Die Rahmen bestehen aus Aluminium. Die Oberlichter liegen auf der Fassadenebene, der untere Teil ist leicht nach vorne versetzt. Durch die Versilberung der Fensterflächen wird eine besondere optische Wirkung erzielt. Die nicht-versilberten Partien blieben durchsichtig und lassen Licht und Blicke ungehindert eindringen. Nur die Eingangstüre ist vollständig durchsichtig; der Türgriff besteht aus einer sehr starken Glasplatte. Über der Türe ist ein Korpus aus Plexiglas angebracht, auf den der Firmenname und ein graphisches Muster auflackiert sind. Abends wird er von zwei starken Spots beleuchtet, die die unzähligen kleinen Spiegelpartikel der Fassade durch die Reflexwirkung hell wie Straßenlampen erstrahlen lassen.

Fassadenlänge            2,65 m
Höhe                     2,70 m

The front of this small hairdresser's has been treated in a most imaginative way that nevertheless harmonizes perfectly with the architecture of the modern building in which it occupies premises.
The frames are aluminium. The upper part of the shop front is in the same plane as the façade of the building, the lower part slightly projecting. The glass is silvered in an elaborate op-art design, the non-silvered parts having been left clear to admit light and enable passers-by to see inside. Only the door with its very thick plate-glass handle is entirely clear.
A plexiglass structure above the door bears the name of the shop and a device painted on it. Two powerful spots illuminate the structure at night, these and the other lights in the street being reflected in the hundreds of little mirrors that make up the composition.

Frontage                 2.65 m
Height                   2.70 m

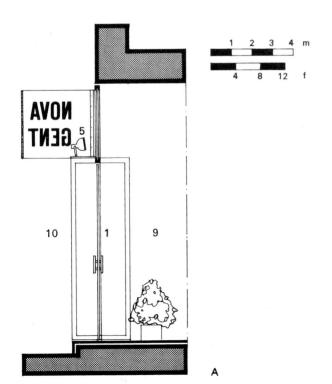

1. La structure en plexiglas surplombant la porte
2. La façade dans sa totalité
3. Un projecteur extérieur
4. La porte d'entrée et la vitrine

1. Der Korpus aus Plexiglas über der Eingangstüre
2. Die Gesamtfassade
3. Ein Außenscheinwerfer
4. Die Eingangstüre und die Vitrine

1. The plexiglass structure above the door
2. View of the whole shop front
3. One of the outside spots
4. The entrance and the display window

1

2

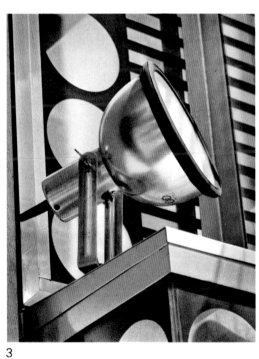

3

4

## 40.  Bugatti, Barcelona          Vincenzo Carmenati Francia, Arch., Milano

Ce magasin de vêtements masculins est situé dans un vaste local occupant le rez-de-chaussée et deux étages d'une maison en pierre. Les volumes de la façade se projettent vers l'extérieur. Ce sont trois tunnels dans lesquels on circule aisément, et dont l'extrémité ouvrant sur la rue est équipée de glaces teintées. Un certain nombre de meurtrières horizontales et verticales permettent en outre la communication visuelle du local sur l'extérieur. La construction est constituée d'une structure en métal, parfois apparente, et d'un habillage réalisé en aluminium anodisé fait de lames successives. Il est à noter que l'ensemble n'est pas perpendiculaire au mur de l'immeuble, mais oblique.

Le petit hall inférieur est ceinturé de vitrines peu profondes; on y trouve aussi la porte d'entrée dont l'ouverture est commandée par cellule photo-électrique. Le revêtement du sol du hall est en plaques de pierre marbrière.

La signalisation structurale ayant été jugée suffisamment généreuse, aucune signalisation lisible importante n'a été mise en place. Seules sur la porte d'entrée des lettres en aluminium indiquent le nom de la maison.

Dieses großräumige Fachgeschäft für Herrenbekleidung nimmt das Erdgeschoß und zwei Stockwerke eines Steinhauses ein. Die in die Fassade eingegliederten Körper ragen weit nach außen vor. Es sind dies drei Tunnels, die von innen begehbar sind und deren der Straßenseite zugewandtes Ende mit farbigem Glas bekleidet ist. Eine Anzahl waagerechter und senkrechter Schlitze ermöglicht eine zusätzliche Sichtverbindung des Lokals nach außen. Die Konstruktion besteht aus einer an manchen Stellen sichtbaren Metallstruktur, mit einer Verkleidung aus eloxiertem Aluminium, die aus gleichförmigen Lamellen zusammengesetzt ist. Es ist bemerkenswert, daß das Ganze nicht im rechten Winkel, sondern schräg zur Wand des Hauses liegt.

Die kleine Halle im Erdgeschoß ist von flachen Vitrinen umgeben; hier befindet sich auch die Eingangstüre, deren Öffnung durch Photozellen gesteuert ist. Der Bodenbelag der Halle besteht aus Marmorwerksteinplatten.

Da die Gastaltung der Fassade hinreichend auffällig ist, verzichtete man auf ein weithin lesbares Firmenschild. Nur auf der Eingangstüre ist der Name des Hauses in Aluminiumbuchstaben angebracht.

This men's clothing shop occupies enormous premises on the ground, first, and second floors of a stone building. The front is distinguished by three projecting volumes. These are tunnels in which one can walk around and of which the ends facing the street are filled with tinted glass. Further visual communication between interior and exterior is provided by a number of vertical slit windows. The structure consists of a metal framework, exposed in places, and a filling of anodized-aluminium strips. A remarkable feature is that the shop front is not in line with the wall of the building but at an angle to it.

The small vestibule is lined with shallow display windows. The door is operated by photo-electric cell. The floor of the vestibule is covered with marbled stone slabs.

The visual impact of the composition is such as to render any large-scale sign superfluous, the name of the shop appearing only on the door, in aluminium lettering.

| Longueur de la façade | 6,50 m | Fassadenlänge | 6,50 m | Frontage | 6.50 m |
| Hauteur | 9,60 m | Höhe | 9,60 m | Height | 9.60 m |

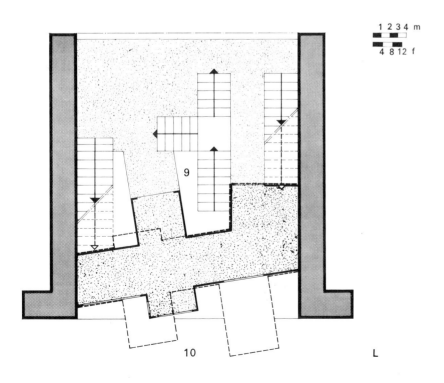

1 2 3 4 m
4 8 12 f

1

2

3. Les structures des tunnels, et en bas, l'amorce des vitrines du hall
4. La projection des tunnels sur la rue
5. L'angle inférieur d'un tunnel

3. Die Struktur der Tunneloberfläche, unten der Ansatz der vor der Halle liegenden Vitrinen
4. Die auf die Straße ragenden Tunnels
5. Die untere Ecke eines Tunnels

3. Looking up at the tunnels, with part of the vestibule display windows below
4. Two of the tunnels project over the pavement
5. Detail of the bottom of one of the tunnels

3 4

6. Le jeu des habillages horizontaux et verticaux en aluminium

6. Spiel der horizontalen und vertikalen Aluminium-verkleidungen

6. The interplay of horizontal and vertical strips in the aluminium filling

5

Une des principales caractéristiques de ce magasin destiné à la vente des revêtements de sol est son hall très vaste, ceinturé de vitrines. Ce hall, bas de plafond, ne comporte aucun angle aigu; il est volontairement très sombre, ce qui confère — par contraste — un éclat particulier à la présentation des articles éclairés. Les vitrines latérales s'intercalent entre les deux arrondis assurant les raccords avec le sol et le plafond. La paroi séparant le hall de l'intérieur est entièrement vitrée. Les deux portes d'accès s'y inscrivent. Le sol, les arrondis inférieurs, les piliers de soutènement et les parties verticales pleines sont revêtus d'un tapis caoutchouté avec des pastilles en relief. Le plafond et les arrondis supérieurs sont réalisés en vinyle épais tendu sur des panneaux de contreplaqué. Les cornières supportant ces panneaux sont métalliques, mais toute la structure générale de la construction est en bois comme le sont les huisseries apparentes. Le plafond du hall étant surbaissé, un rideau métallique à mailles a pu être installé. Il se déroule près du pilier côté rue. La façade proprement dite en légère avancée sur le mur de l'immeuble est entièrement réalisée en carreaux de céramique vernissée.
Les lettres de la raison sociale sont des tubes néon; leur lecture est aussi évidente le jour que la nuit.

Eines der Hauptmerkmale dieses Fachgeschäfts für Bodenbeläge ist seine großzügige, von Schaufenstern eingerahmte Halle. Diese mit einer niedrigen Decke ausgestattete Halle enthält nur abgerundete Ecken; sie ist bewußt sehr dunkel gehalten, wodurch ein effektvoller Kontrast zu der ausgestellten, sehr stark beleuchteten Ware entsteht. Die seitlichen Schaufenster fügen sich zwischen die beiden abgerundeten Wandflächen ein, die die Verbindung mit dem Fußboden und der Decke herstellen. Die Trennwand zwischen der Halle und dem Innenbereich besteht ganz aus Glas und enthält die beiden Eingangstüren. Der Boden, die unteren Wandrundungen, die Stützpfeiler und die senkrechten Füllflächen sind mit einem gummierten Belag mit Noppenstruktur verkleidet. Die Decke und die oberen Wandrundungen sind in Furnierplatten mit einer starken Vinylbeschichtung ausgeführt. Diese Plattenstruktur wird von metallenen Winkeleisen getragen, die gesamte übrige Unterkonstruktion besteht jedoch aus Holz wie auch die freiliegenden Rahmen. Aufgrund der niedrigen Hallendecke konnte ein metallisches Schutzgitter angebracht werden. Es wird von dem an der Straßenseite liegenden Stützpfeiler her ausgerollt. Die Geschäftsfassade springt etwas vor und ist ganz mit glasierten Keramikfliesen verkleidet.
Die Buchstaben des Firmennamens bestehen aus Neonröhren, so daß die Schrift tags und nachts gleich augenfällig ist.

One of the most distinctive features of this flooring-materials shop is an enormous low-ceilinged gallery lined with display windows. This gallery, which contains no sharp angles, is kept deliberately dark in order to lend, by contrast, added brilliance to the brightly-lit displays. Above and below the side windows the transitions to ceiling and floor respectively are curved. The partition between gallery and shop, including the two doors, is entirely glazed. The floor (with the curve up to the bottom of the windows), the supporting pillars, and the solid vertical portions are covered with rubber matting with a pastille relief. The ceiling (with the curve above the windows) is covered with thick vinyl stretched on plywood panels. With the exception of the angle-irons supporting these panels the entire structure, including the exposed frames, is executed in wood. The fact that the gallery ceiling is dropped meant that a metal security curtain could be housed above it. This comes down near the pillar towards the street. The actual shop front, which projects slightly from the wall of the building, is completely covered with varnished ceramic tiling.
The lettering is done in neon tubing and is equally legible day and night.

| Longueur de la façade | 8 m |
| Hauteur | 3,85 m |
| Profondeur du hall | 5,50 m |

| Fassadenlänge | 8 m |
| Höhe | 3,85 m |
| Tiefe der Halle | 5,50 m |

| Frontage | 8 m |
| Height | 3.85 m |
| Depth of gallery | 5.50 m |

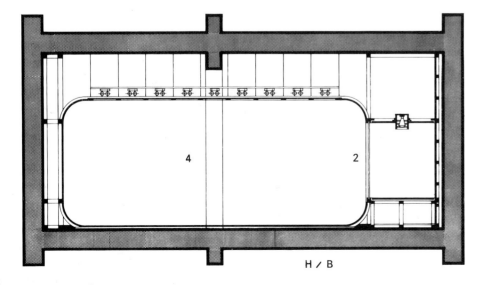

H / B

1. La façade
2. Les arrondis sol-plafond et une amorce de vitrine
3. Le hall vu de l'intérieur du magasin

1. Die Fassade
2. Die gerundeten Wandflächen vom Boden zur Decke und das Ansatzstück einer Vitrine
3. Die Halle vom Inneren des Geschäfts aus gesehen

1. View of the whole shop front
2. The curved floor/wall and wall/ceiling transitions and part of a display window
3. The gallery from inside the shop

2   3

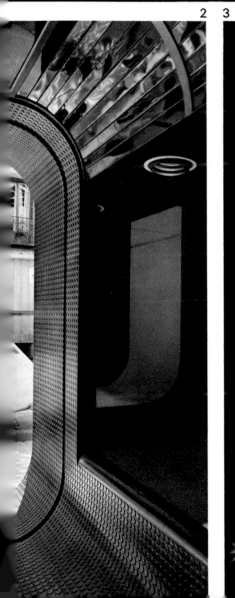

4

5

7

6

4. Les lames minces tendues de vinyle formant l'arrondi
   supérieur
5. L'angle inférieur et les carreaux de la façade
6. Le rail du rideau de protection inscrit dans le revêtement de caoutchouc
7. La partie inférieure d'un battant de la porte d'entrée

4. Die schmalen, vinylbeschichteten Platten der oberen
   Wandrundung
5. Die untere Ecke und die Fliesenbekleidung der
   Fassade
6. Die in die Gummiverkleidung eingelassene Schiene
   des Schutzgitters
7. Der untere Teil eines Flügels der Eingangstüre

4. The thin strips of stretched vinyl forming the upper
   curve
5. Detail of the bottom corner and the tiling of the
   façade
6. The rubber floor and wall covering, showing the rail
   for the security curtain
7. Detail of the lower part of the door

8

8.  La façade et le hall de nuit

8.  Ansicht der Fassade und der Halle bei Nacht

8.  The shop front and the gallery at night

## 42. Flash, Barcelona

A. Mila, F. Correa, Arch., Barcelona

Un restaurant n'a pas forcément besoin de vitrines de présentation, bien que pendant le jour la lumière naturelle soit tout de même appréciée par la clientèle. Le principe a été respecté pour cette réalisation. La façade proprement dite et la double porte d'entrée en léger retrait sont réalisées en glace claire, les huisseries en métal laqué. A quelques centimètres en arrière, une construction très économique en bois est percée d'ouvertures circulaires. Les parties pleines sont entièrement habillées d'un papier photographique à fond blanc où se détachent la signalisation et des agrandissements de silhouettes donnant le ton très jeune et dynamique de l'établissement. Un bandeau lumineux horizontal longe la vitrine, extérieurement. En outre, de vrais spots électroniques intégrés à ceux des agrandissements photographiques projettent des éclairs de signalisation. Les photos ont été réalisées par L. Pomes.

Ein Restaurant braucht nicht unbedingt mit Schaufenstern ausgestattet zu sein, obwohl der Gast gern Tageslicht hat. Dieser Gesichtspunkt wurde hier berücksichtigt. Die Fassadenwand und die etwas zurückgesetzte, zweiflügelige Eingangstüre bestehen aus Glas, die Rahmen aus lackiertem Metall. Wenige Zentimeter dahinter befindet sich eine einfache Holzkonstruktion mit kreisförmigen Ausschnitten. Die Füllflächen sind ganz mit weißgrundigem Photopapier verkleidet, auf dem der Firmenname sowie vergrößerte Silhouetten zu sehen sind, die den jugendlichen und dynamischen Stil des Lokals betonen. Außen läuft am Schaufenster ein waagerechtes Lichtband entlang. Darüberhinaus senden elektronische Spots, die in die Photovergrößerungen eingesetzt sind, Lichtsignale aus. Die Photos stammen von L. Pomes.

A restaurant does not *have* to have display windows although of course customers do appreciate eating by daylight during the daytime. In this case the principle has been retained. The actual front and the slightly recessed double doors are of clear glass, the framing of enamelled metal. A few centimetres behind this is an extremely economical wooden structure pierced with circular apertures. The solid portions are covered with photographic paper on which the name of the establishment and three enlarged silhouettes projecting a young, dynamic image stand out against a white ground. A fitting with strip lights runs the whole length of the front. Actual electronic spots fitted in the 'flashlights' of the photographic enlargements beam an invitation at passers-by. The photos were taken by L. Pomes.

| | | | | |
|---|---|---|---|---|
| Longueur de la façade | 8,30 m | Fassadenlänge | 8,30 m | Frontage | 8.30 m |
| Hauteur | 2,80 m | Höhe | 2,80 m | Height | 2.80 m |

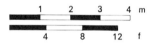

B

**1**

1. La façade; à droite, le sas d'accès
2. La vitrine et son bandeau lumineux
3. L'angle de la façade vers le sas d'accès

1. Die Fassade, rechts die Eingangszone
2. Die Vitrine mit dem darüberliegenden Lichtband
3. Die Ecke der Fassade in Richtung auf die Eingangszone gesehen

1. View of the front, showing the recessed entrance on the right
2. The windows and the horizontal strip-light fitting
3. The corner of the front, looking towards the entrance

**2**

**3**

Le volume de ce magasin d'articles de sports s'élève sur deux niveaux dans un immeuble actuel où domine la brique naturelle. En opposition aux longues horizontales de l'architecture, la façade est composée verticalement. Pour accuser ce parti esthétique, ce sont les huisseries en bois laqué encadrant la porte, son imposte en glace et les vitrines qui sont déterminantes, mais aussi le fût d'un signal dont une partie perpendiculaire déborde largement de la façade. L'intérieur de ce signal, réalisé en bois, est creux. Ceci a permis d'y installer un éclairage et d'y découper les lettres de la raison sociale, ainsi que le graphisme de la marque. La porte et une des vitrines sont en retrait de la façade de l'immeuble. Dans le petit sas extérieur ainsi créé prennent place des plantes vertes qui animent la rigueur de la composition. Le sol de ce sas et le seuil de la vitrine voisine sont le prolongement du revêtement du sol intérieur, constitué de plaques de marbre aggloméré.

Dieses Sportgeschäft liegt auf zwei Geschossen in einem modernen Gebäude, in dem der Backstein dominiert. Die Geschäftsfassade ist im Gegensatz zu den langgezogenen Horizontalen der Architektur vertikal ausgerichtet. Bestimmend für diesen ästhetischen Eindruck sind die Türrahmen aus lackiertem Metall, die Verglasung über der Türe und die Schaufenster, ebenso jedoch der Schaft eines signalartigen Firmenschildes, dessen rechtwinklig abgebogener Teil weit vorspringt. Dieses hölzerne Firmenschild ist innen hohl. Dadurch konnte eine Innenbeleuchtung installiert und der Firmenname sowie das Markenzeichen ausgestanzt werden. Die Eingangstüre und eines der Schaufenster sind hinter die Gebäudefassade zurückgesetzt. Der dadurch entstandene kleine Vorraum im Freien ist mit Grünpflanzen ausgestattet, die die strenge Komposition beleben. Der Boden des Vorraums und das Sims der anschließenden Vitrine bilden die Fortführung des Bodenbelags im Inneren, der aus Marmorplatten besteht.

This sports-equipment shop occupies premises on two floors of a modern building in which the dominant material is brick. In contrast to the extended horizontals of the architecture the shop front is composed vertically. Decisive in this respect are not only the painted wooden uprights flanking the door, the transom window above it, and the display windows, but also the shaft of the sign supporting an arm that projects at right angles to the shop front. This sign, also made of wood, is hollow inside and accommodates a lamp illuminating the firm's name and device cut in the sides. The door and one of the display windows are set back from the line of the façade, leaving a small vestibule with green plants that have the effect of enlivening an otherwise severe composition. The floor of the vestibule and the sill of the adjacent display window represent a continuation of the floor of the shop and are done in the same slabs of marble agglomerate.

| Longueur de la façade | 4,30 m |
| Hauteur | 5,40 m |

| Fassadenlänge | 4,30 m |
| Höhe | 5,40 m |

| Frontage | 4.30 m |
| Height | 5.40 m |

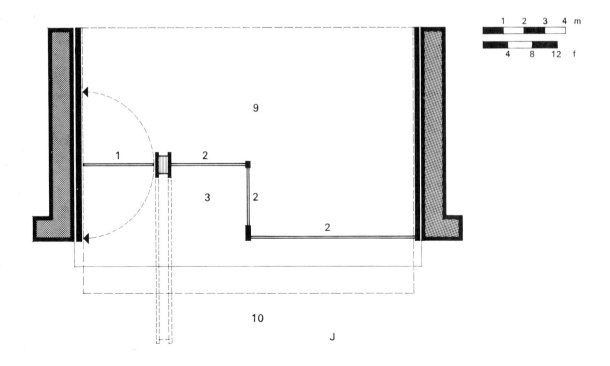

1

2

1. La façade vue de face
2. L'enseigne se projetant sur la rue
3. L'enseigne-signal dans la composition générale

1. Frontalansicht der Fassade
2. Das auf die Straße hinausragende Firmenschild
3. Das signalartige Firmenschild in der Gesamtkomposition

1. General view of the shop front
2. The sign projecting over the pavement
3. The sign in the context of the general composition 3

4

5

4.  Le signal vu de l'intérieur du magasin
5. 6.  Le sas extérieur et la porte d'entrée

4.  Das Schild vom Ladeninneren her gesehen
5. 6.  Der äußere Vorraum und die Eingangstüre

4.  The sign from inside the shop
5. 6.  The vestibule and the door

Ce magasin de mode masculine est situé à l'angle de deux rues dont une est très animée. La façade, tout en étant homogène et globale, présente deux physionomies distinctes. Le plus petit côté s'ouvre sur la rue principale. Il est équipé de glace claire (vitrine et porte d'entrée). Cette glace est inscrite dans une structure en avancée sur le mur de l'immeuble, comme le bandeau surmontant l'ensemble. Structure et bandeau sont en acier inoxydable. Le côté le plus long présente une alternance de pleins et de vides. Les parties pleines dont le profil présente deux pans coupés ont été traitées en bois, puis laquées. Les vitrines en léger retrait ne vont pas jusqu'au sol; elles sont montées dans des huisseries métalliques et barrées à hauteur d'appui par des tubes chromés.
Le nom de la maison se détache en lettres lumineuses (face en plexiglas) sur le plein le plus large, perpendiculaire à la façade d'entrée; en outre, les éclairs de plusieurs lampes-flash, alignées sur les lettres ou intégrées au bandeau inox, attirent le regard dès que tombe la nuit.

Dieses Herrenmodengeschäft liegt am Schnittpunkt zweier Straßen, deren eine sehr belebt ist. Die Fassade zeigt trotz ihres homogenen und durchkomponierten Eindrucks zwei verschiedene Gesichter. Die kleinere Fassadenseite ist der Hauptstraße zugewandt. Sie besteht aus Schaufensterglas (Vitrine und Eingangstüre). Das Glas ist in ein Rahmengestell eingesetzt, das wie die obere Fassadenblende von der Gebäudefront absteht. Gestell und Blende bestehen aus nichtrostendem Stahl. Die längere Fassadenseite ist abwechselnd in durchsichtige und undurchsichtige Flächen gegliedert. Die undurchsichtigen Flächen zeigen im Profil zwei schräge Fassadenelemente und bestehen aus lackiertem Holz. Die leicht zurückgesetzten Vitrinen reichen nicht bis ganz zum Boden hinunter und sind in Metallrahmen eingesetzt; auf Geländerhöhe verläuft eine Barriere aus Chromstangen.
Auf der größten, im rechten Winkel zur Fassadenseite des Eingangs gelegenen Füllfläche ist der Name des Hauses in Leuchtbuchstaben angebracht (Vorderseite aus Plexiglas). Mit Einbruch der Dunkelheit werden ferner mehrere Blinklampen eingeschaltet; sie sind in die nichtrostende Fassadenblende eingelassen und strahlen den Firmennamen an, der so die Blicke auf sich lenkt.

This men's fashion shop is situated on the corner of two streets, one of them extremely busy. The shop front, while presenting a homogeneous whole, nevertheless has two distinct faces. The smaller front is on the busier street. It consists of a clear-glass display window and door framed by a structure that, like the facia surmounting the whole, projects slightly from the façade of the building. Structure and facia are executed in stainless steel. The longer front offers a series of alternate solids and spaces. The solid portions, consisting of two canted surfaces, are made of wood and painted. The slightly recessed display windows stop before they reach the ground. They are mounted in metal frames and have chromium-plated bars running across them at hand-height.
The name of the shop stands out in luminous letters (fronted with plexiglass) that are cut in the largest solid surface at right angles to the entrance front. Further visual attraction at night is provided by a number of flashlights housed in the stainless-steel facia and aligned with the lettering.

| | | | |
|---|---|---|---|
| Longueur de la façade | 10,60 m | Fassadenlänge | 10,60 m |
| Hauteur | 2,70 m | Höhe | 2,70 m |

| | |
|---|---|
| Frontage | 10.60 m |
| Height | 2.70 m |

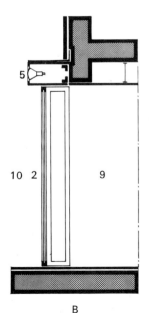

1. L'enseigne et les lampes-flash sur la façade latérale
2. La façade de l'entrée

1. Das Firmenschild und die Blinklampen auf der Seitenfassade
2. Die Fassadenseite mit dem Eingang

1. The sign and the flashlights in the side front
2. The entrance front

1

2

3

4

3. La façade la plus longue
4. L'ensemble à l'angle des deux artères
5. 6. Les lampes-flash aux deux angles du bandeau
7. La structure de la vitrine en avancée
8. L'angle inférieur d'une des vitrines latérales et sa barre d'appui

3. Die längere Fassadenseite
4. Die Anlage am Schnittpunkt der beiden Straßen
5. 6. Die Blinklampen an den beiden Ecken der nichtrostenden Fassadenblende
7. Das Gestell der vorgezogenen Vitrine
8. Die untere Ecke eines der seitlichen Schaufenster und die Geländerstange

3. The longer of the two fronts
4. The shop occupies a corner site
5. 6. The flashlights on the corners of the stainless-steel facia
7. The structure of the projecting display window
8. The bottom corner of one of the side windows, showing the hand-rail

5

6

7

8

Enseignes          Firmenschilder          Signs

Il est impensable de concevoir une façade de magasin anonyme, sans aucun signal, sans aucune enseigne. Si tel était le cas, l'impact du magasin sur la clientèle potentielle en serait dangereusement amoindri.

L'enseigne s'adresse à deux regards:
— Le regard du client habitué ou conseillé, informé par les moyens publicitaires actuels et qui aime trouver rapidement dans la juxtaposition des magasins celui qui l'intéresse.
— Le regard du promeneur, du badaud, qui, séduit, viendra contempler les produits et pourra ainsi les localiser dans sa mémoire grâce à une raison sociale, un nom, un graphisme.

Avec l'affiche et la vitrine, l'enseigne participe à l'animation de la rue qui, sans elles, serait le plus souvent banale, et toujours triste.
Chaque magasin a donc en principe une enseigne appropriée, mais il est impossible de conseiller en matière d'emplacement préférentiel, comme il est imprévisible de connaître à l'avance les réactions inconscientes que vont déclencher la lecture de certains noms ou d'associations de mots, l'appréciation esthétique des lettres, labels et sigles. Chaque type de clientèle réagit différemment. C'est une affaire de marketing sinon de bon sens.
Toutes les contingences, tous les problèmes exposés dans le texte d'introduction se retrouvent ici. En schématisant, il est possible de dire qu'une enseigne peut être placée sur le même plan que la façade ou sur un plan perpendiculaire par rapport à celle-ci.
Pour chaque cas, voici une liste simplifiée des solutions pratiques les plus couramment adoptées.

1) L'enseigne est placée sur le même plan que la façade

— Les éléments (lettres, graphismes, sigles) sont peints sur un fond opaque pouvant être la façade elle-même, ou des panneaux plus ou moins en relief (voir pp. 75 et 165).

— Les éléments sont peints, imprimés ou en relief sur des fonds translucides faisant partie de la façade ou rapportés en saillie (caissons). Ces fonds sont éclairés par l'arrière.

— Les éléments sont peints sur les vitrines (voir p. 69).

— Les éléments sont en relief, appliqués ou décollés du fond et réalisés dans un matériau opaque.

Eine anonyme Geschäftsfassade ohne irgendein Signal, ohne irgendein Firmenschild ist undenkbar. In einem solchen Fall wäre die Wirkung auf die potentielle Kundschaft gefährlich beeinträchtigt.

Das Firmenschild wendet sich an zwei verschiedene Betrachter:
— An den Stammkunden oder den versierten Kunden, der durch die modernen Medien informiert ist und unter den nebeneinanderliegenden Geschäften schnell dasjenige herausfinden will, das ihn interessiert.
— An den Spaziergänger und Bummler, der zur Betrachtung der Schaufensterauslagen verführt wird und sie sich anhand einer Firmenbezeichnung, eines Namens, eines Schriftzuges, einprägen kann.

Neben dem Plakat und dem Schaufenster trägt auch das Firmenschild zur Belebung des Straßenbildes bei, das ohne sie meistens phantasielos und trist aussehen würde.
Jedes Geschäft hat daher grundsätzlich sein eigenes Firmenschild, doch ist es unmöglich, einen Rat hinsichtlich der günstigsten Anbringung zu geben, ebenso wie die unbewußten Reaktionen kaum vorhersehbar sind, die durch die Lektüre bestimmter Namen oder Wortassoziationen, sowie durch die ästhetische Wirkung bestimmter Buchstaben, Firmenzeichen und Symbole hervorgerufen werden. Jede Kategorie von Käufern reagiert anders. Es ist eine Sache der Marktforschung, wenn nicht einfach des gesunden Menschenverstandes.
Alle Kriterien und Probleme, die in der Einführung dargelegt wurden, sind auch hier relevant. Theoretisch kann gesagt werden, daß ein Firmenschild entweder auf derselben Ebene wie die Fassade oder auf einer im rechten Winkel dazu liegenden Ebene angebracht werden soll.
Für jede der beiden Möglichkeiten wird hier eine vereinfachte Liste der praktischen Lösungen aufgeführt, die am häufigsten anzutreffen sind.

1) Das Firmenschild liegt auf der Ebene der Fassade

— Die Elemente des Firmenschildes (Buchstaben, graphische Zeichen, Symbole) sind auf einen undurchsichtigen Hintergrund aufgemalt, der entweder die Fassade selbst sein kann, oder in Form mehr oder weniger plastisch hervortretender Platten erscheint (siehe S. 75 und 165).

— Die Elemente sind auf durchsichtige Flächen aufgemalt oder aufgedruckt, die entweder Be-

A completely anonymous shop front without any kind of sign whatever is inconceivable. If such a shop front did exist, its impact on potential customers would be dangerously reduced.

The sign is aimed at two kinds of eye:
— that of the regular customer, or the customer to whom the shop has been recommended or who has read about it or seen an advertisement. Faced with a row of shops, he wants to be able to pick out quickly the one he is interested in;
— that of the casual passer-by who, attracted by it, will approach and have a look at the products, which he will then be able to 'place' in his memory thanks to a particular device or slogan or name.

Signs, together with posters and shop windows, contribute to the liveliness of our streets, which without them would be frequently banal and invariably depressing.
In principle, then, every shop will have a particular sign that is suited to it, but it is as impossible to give advice about the best place to put it as it is to predict the unconscious reactions that certain names or combinations of words will prompt in the minds of passers-by or their aesthetic reactions to particular kinds of lettering and graphic art. Each type of clientele reacts differently. It is a question of marketing, but above all it is a question of common sense.
All the contingencies and problems mentioned in the course of the introduction apply here as well. Summing up, we can say that a sign may be placed either in the same plane as the shop front or at right angles to that plane. Taking each case in turn, here is a brief survey of the most commonly adopted practical solutions.

1) The sign is in the same plane as the shop front

— The elements of the sign (lettering, graphics, etc.) are painted on an opaque background that may be the shop front itself or panels in a greater or lesser degree of relief (see pp. 75 and 165).

— The elements are painted, printed, or in relief on translucent backgrounds forming part of the shop front or projecting from it (boxes), these being then illuminated from behind.

— The elements are painted on the shop window (see p. 69).

— The elements are executed in some opaque material that is either applied to or stands out from the

SOLDECOR

BLAUPUNKT

Lorsqu'ils sont décollés du fond, ils peuvent contenir un éclairage nocturne qui les cernera d'une lumière diffuse (voir pp. 23, 47 et 83).

— Les éléments sont en relief et réalisés dans des matériaux translucides et éclairés de l'intérieur. Certaines parties métalliques assurent la rigidité de l'ensemble et permettent quelquefois des pleins opaques (voir pp. 99 et 137).

— Les éléments sont réalisés en néon, ou par alignement ou groupements de lampes incandescentes (voir pp. 161 et 163).

— Les éléments sont découpés (en réserve) dans des panneaux opaques décollés de fonds lumineux ou non (voir pp. 125, 129 et 171).

Ces diverses formules se combinent à l'infini. A titre de seul exemple: on peut envisager des lettres en acier cernées de néon ou l'inverse (voir pp. 95 et 97). Lorsque l'éclairage ne fait pas partie intégrante de l'enseigne, les faisceaux lumineux prévus doivent être orientés avec soin (voir pp. 74 et 75).

*2) L'enseigne est perpendiculaire ou oblique par rapport à la façade*

— Si le texte est court et si les éléments qui le composent sont de taille réduite, il sera lu selon la tradition, horizontalement.
— Si le texte est long et les éléments importants, il s'étalera verticalement.

Toutes les formules précédentes peuvent être reprises ici (voir pp. 27 et 28). Mais les enseignes perpendiculaires, et principalement celles qui sont verticales, étant surtout destinées à être vues la nuit, elles seront réalisées de préférence en relief dans un matériau translucide avec éclairage intérieur, peintes sur des caissons présentant les mêmes caractéristiques, ou en tube de néon, en groupement de lampes incandescentes.

Les matériaux les plus usités dans la fabrication des enseignes sont: l'acier, inoxydable ou peint, le cuivre, le verre, le perspex, l'altuglass, le bois. Aucun matériau n'est cependant à proscrire si la fabrication en est soignée, conçue pour résister à la détérioration des eaux de pluie. L'équipement électrique doit présenter une sécurité totale. Toutes les combinaisons d'allumages peuvent être programmées et minutées.

standteil der Fassade oder auf die Fassade aufgesetzt sind (Kästen). Diese Flächen werden von hinten erleuchtet.

— Die Elemente sind auf die Schaufenster aufgemalt (siehe S. 69).

— Die Elemente sind plastisch, direkt auf den Hintergrund aufgesetzt oder davon abgehoben, und bestehen aus einem undurchsichtigen Material. Wenn sie vom Hintergrund abgehoben sind, können sie mit einer Beleuchtung für die Nacht ausgestattet sein, die sie mit einem diffusen Lichtschein umgibt (siehe S. 23, 47 und 83).

— Die Elemente sind plastisch, in durchsichtigem Material ausgeführt und mit einer Innenbeleuchtung ausgestattet. Einige Partien aus Metall geben dem Gesamtbild schärfere Konturen und schaffen gegebenenfalls undurchsichtige Flächen (siehe S. 99 und 137).

— Die Elemente bestehen aus Neonröhren oder aus aneinandergereihten bzw. gruppierten Glühbirnen (siehe S. 161 und 163).

— Die Elemente sind aus undurchsichtigen Flächen ausgestanzt, die sich vor einem leuchtenden oder auch unauffälligen Hintergrund abheben (siehe S. 125, 129 und 171).

Diese verschiedenen Formeln können ins Unendliche miteinander kombiniert werden. Einziges konkretes Beispiel: Man wählt etwa Buchstaben aus Stahl mit einer Umrandung aus Neonröhren oder umgekehrt (siehe S. 95 und 97). Wenn die Beleuchtung nicht integrierender Bestandteil des Firmenschildes ist, müssen die vorgesehenen Lichtbündel sorgfältig ausgerichtet werden (siehe S. 74 und 75).

*2) Das Firmenschild liegt schräg oder im rechten Winkel zur Fassade*

— Wenn der Text kurz ist und die Elemente, aus denen er sich zusammensetzt, einen beschränkten Umfang aufweisen, soll er traditionsgemäß waagerecht zu lesen sein.

— Ist der Text lang und beinhaltet er umfangreiche Elemente, ordnet man ihn besser senkrecht an.

Alle oben aufgeführten Formeln haben auch hier Gültigkeit (siehe S. 27 und 28). Die rechtwinklig

background. When they stand out from the background they can contain light fittings that will bathe them in diffused lighting at night (see pp. 23, 47 and 83).

— The elements are executed in relief in some translucent material and lit from within. Metal parts ensure the rigidity of the whole and can provide the occasional opaque area (see pp. 99 and 137).

— The elements are executed in neon tubing or in light bulbs fixed in lines or clusters (see pp. 161 and 163).

— The elements are cut out of opaque panels that can be made to stand out against a luminous background or not, as required (see pp. 125, 129 and 171).

These different solutions can be combined in any number of ways. To take just one example, lettering executed in steel can be outlined with neon tubing, or the other way round (see pp. 95 and 97). When some form of lighting does not form an integral part of the sign, the lighting beamed on the shop front must be very carefully aimed (see pp. 74-5).

*2) The sign projects at right angles or at an oblique angle to the shop front*

— If the text is a short one and the elements that make it up are kept small, it can be read in the traditional manner, i.e. horizontally.
— A long text made up of large-scale elements will be aligned vertically.

All the solutions mentioned above are applicable here as well (see pp. 27-8). But since signs standing at right angles to the shop front, and in particular those that read vertically, are primarily designed to be seen at night, they will be best executed in relief in some translucent material lit from inside, or painted on translucent boxes likewise lit from inside, or done in neon or in arrangements of light bulbs.

The materials most commonly used in the manufacture of signs are steel (stainless or painted), copper, glass, perspex, altuglass, and wood. In fact, though, any material may be used, provided that it is carefully worked and designed to stand up

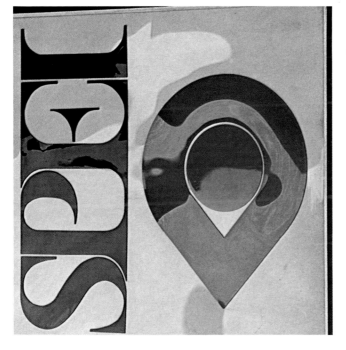

Ainsi dans la composition d'une façade, dans la répartition des pleins et des vides, dans le jeu des proportions générales, l'enseigne trouve une place de choix, titre et signature à la fois.

zur Fassade liegenden Firmenschilder und insbesondere die senkrecht angeordneten sind indessen vor allem auf die Wirkung bei Nacht angelegt und sollen daher vorzugsweise plastisch und in einem durchsichtigen Material mit Innenbeleuchtung ausgeführt sein, oder auch auf Kästen aufgemalt, die diese Eigenschaften aufweisen, oder schließlich ganz aus Neonröhren oder auch in Gruppen angeordneten Glühbirnen bestehen.

Die gebräuchlichsten Materialien für Firmenschilder sind: Stahl (nichtrostend oder gestrichen), Kupfer, Glas, Kunststoff, Plexiglas, Holz.
Es kann jedoch jedes andere Material verwendet werden, vorausgesetzt, es wird sorgfältig verarbeitet und hält den Witterungsschäden durch Regenwasser stand. Die elektrischen Installationen müssen allen Sicherheitsanforderungen restlos genügen. Alle Beleuchtungskombinationen können programmiert und mit einer Schaltuhr geregelt werden.

So findet das Firmenschild in der Komposition einer Fassade, in der Verteilung freier und ausgefüllter Flächen, im Spiel der Gesamtproportionen einen bevorzugten Platz und wird Repräsentant und Markenzeichen in einem.

to the weather. Light fittings must be made completely safe. All the above-mentioned lighting variants can be programmed and made to operate automatically.

With regard to the general composition of the shop front, the distribution of solids and spaces, and the play of the overall proportions, the sign will occupy a choice place, filling the twin roles of title and signature.

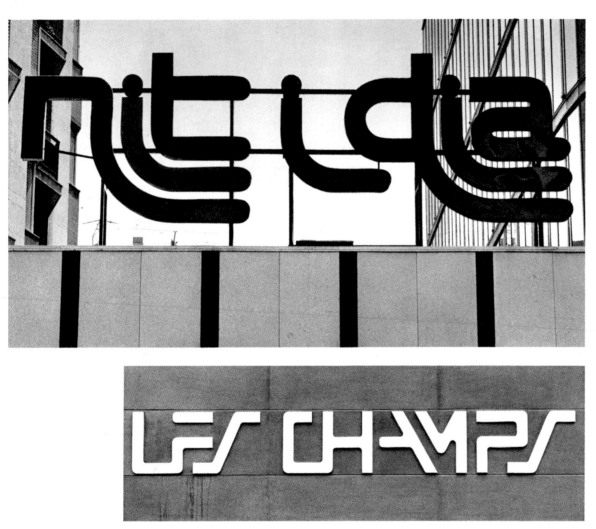

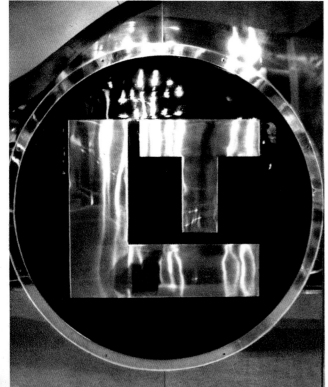

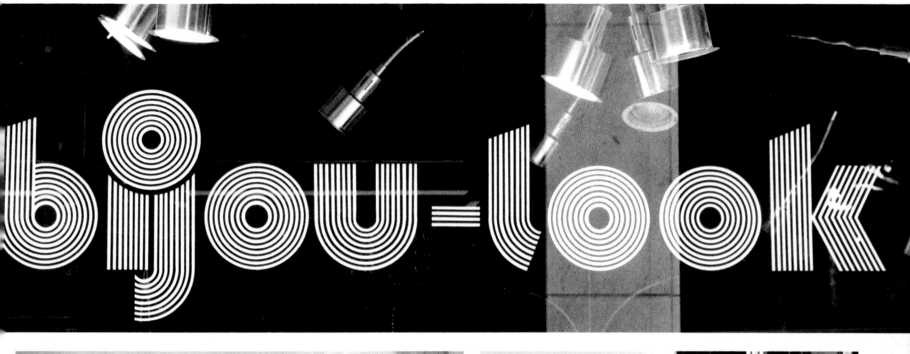

plans

Legenden der Pläne

Key to the plans

Les photos qui n'ont pas été réalisées par Michel Nahmias, Paris, proviennent de:

Brecht-Einzig Limited, London: p. 55; Jacques Debaigts, Paris: pp. 37 n° 1, 38, 177 (Orange, Soldecor, Blaupunkt), 181 (U), 191 (Guida), 192 (MF); Colorphoto Hans Hinz, Basel: pp. 179 (Hotel Drachen), 184 (Kino-Snackbar, Merkur Tricot), 185 (car+driver), 192 (Magmod, Hermann Miller, Möbel Roesch); Eric Lieuré, Paris: pp. 23-25; Torben Thesander, Copenhagen: pp. 71, 73-75.

Cet ouvrage a été achevé d'imprimer en août 1974 par Roto-Sadag S.A., Genève, pour le texte, les illustrations et la jaquette en quatre couleurs offset, et les reproductions en héliogravure. — Les photolithos proviennent de la maison Atesa Argraf S.A., Genève. — La reliure a été effectuée par les ateliers Roger Veihl, Genève. — Secrétariat de rédaction: Dominique Guisan. — Secrétariat de production: Suzanne Meister.

Printed in Switzerland